THE DANCE OF DEATH

THE DANCE OF DEATH

AUGUST STRINDBERG

Translated

by

NORMAN GINSBURY

MINNEAPOLIS

Cornelius Publishers

1966

TYRONE GUTHRIE THEATRE EDITIONS

Books in the 1966 Series

AS YOU LIKE IT	WILLIAM SHAKESPEARE
THE SKIN OF OUR TEETH	THORNTON WILDER
THE DANCE OF DEATH	AUGUST STRINDBERG
THE DOCTOR'S DILEMMA	BERNARD SHAW
S.S. GLENCAIRN	EUGENE O'NEILL

Plays Produced by the Minnesota Theatre Company

FIRST EDITION

Copyright © 1966 by Norman Ginsbury

Library of Congress Catalog Card Number: 66-20323

Copyright © 1966 by Cornelius Publishers, Minneapolis.
Printed in the United States of America

PREFACE

August Strindberg was born in Stockholm in January, 1849. He died
there in May, 1912. His first play, IN ROME, was produced when he
was twenty-one. In the remaining forty-two years of his life, he created
paintings, essays, short stories, novels, poems and plays: plays historical, plays mystical, plays naturalistic, plays supernaturalistic, plays
avant-garde.

Strindberg's life was one of violent contradictions. He was a
plebeian, a revolutionary, a socialist who believed in Nietzsche's
superman and who regarded himself as a superman. He turned from
God to atheism and back again to God. He was a paranoiac whose
persecution mania lost him his friends and at times drove him beyond
sanity. He was, in turn, execrated and idolized by the public. He was
a woman-hater who could not live without women. To him, women
were "the necessary evil." His three marriages were failures. He loved
his wives and he loathed them. Most of all, he loved and loathed the
first one, the actress Siri von Essen, whom he married in 1877 after
she divorced his friend, Baron Wrangel.

The love-hate of the sexes became a constantly repeated theme in
Strindberg's writings. They overflowed with Freudian ideas years before Freud was understood or appreciated. His anti-feminist views
became more and more virulent and when Ibsen's feminist play, A
DOLL'S HOUSE, appeared in 1879, Strindberg detested it. Women, to
him, were the female spiders who devoured their mates. In THE FATHER,
written in 1887, he gives us a terrifying picture of a husband helpless
in the web of his fiendish, scheming wife, Laura. The play was written

when his first marriage was breaking up and he poured into it a hatred and a venom that is rare in literature. Laura, of course, is Siri, but a Siri distorted by Strindberg's fevered imagination. Tekla, the faithless woman of THE CREDITORS, written the next year, is Siri again. MISS JULIE was also written in 1889. The pathetic, man-hating, hungry-for-men Julie is yet another vision of Siri.

For several years after the end of his marriage to Siri, he produced no plays of importance. Then came a glut of them including the first two parts of TO DAMASCUS, which combines mysticism, symbolism, naturalism and supernaturalism; CRIMES AND CRIMES, which deals with conscience, guilt and self-punishment; and a series of historical plays influenced in part by Shakespeare. EASTER, a gentle, moving play about redemption and the power of love, and THE DANCE OF DEATH followed in 1901. By then, Strindberg's second marriage (to the Austrian writer, Frida Uhl) had come to an end and he had just taken a third wife, Harriet Bosse, another actress.

THE DANCE OF DEATH marks a return to naturalism and morbidity. Its ferocity and malevolence outdo anything he had written previously. In its mounting horror, nothing except perhaps Ibsen's GHOSTS compares with it. Strindberg has gone back to his old theme. It is the war of the sexes again but in this case, the husband, Edgar, is at least a match for his wife, Alice. It is demon fighting demon and each of them is merciless. "It is love-hate and it comes from hell." Edgar is, in part, Strindberg himself. So is Kurt, whose conscience is at war with his sensuality and whose "What would people say?" was an expression constantly dinned into the young Strindberg's ears. Alice, the retired actress, with exaggerated views of her histrionic potential, is poor Siri all over again.

Part I ends with a reconciliation but in Part II, the hatred is dominant again. This, the shorter half, is relieved by the introduction of the love-sick Allan, Judith and the Lieutenant, all of them portrayed with charm and tenderness. At the end, when Alice's hopes are fulfilled and Edgar is dead, when she has thanked God for delivering her from "this evil," when she can look forward, in her remaining years, to peace and tranquillity, the image of her husband as the eager, young man with whom she had fallen in love, comes back to her. "I saw him, I can see him now, as he was when he was twenty years old. . . . I must have loved that man.'. . . And hated. God rest his soul." It is suffering, she realizes, not happiness, that is permanent.

It pleased Strindberg to think he was influencing his contemporaries. (He believed that Ibsen's HEDDA GABLER had been fashioned out of his Laura of THE FATHER and his Tekla of THE CREDITORS.) More than half a century later, his work still holds the stage. His naturalistic plays have not dated; his avant-garde plays are startlingly avant-garde.

NORMAN GINSBURY

I wish to thank Mrs. Ingela Dietz for her valuable collaboration in preparing this translation and Mr. Cyril Glynn of the Ny Teater, Copenhagen, for his expert scrutiny and criticisms.

N.G.

THE DANCE OF DEATH

PART I

CHARACTERS

EDGAR, *in command of the fortress*

ALICE, *his wife, previously an actress*

KURT, *in charge of the Quarantine Station*

JENNY, *a servant*

AN OLD WOMAN

A SENTRY *(mute)*

The interior of a round granite fortress on an island off the coast of Sweden. At back, centre, is the entrance, a great gateway with glass doors. Beyond is the seashore with battery.

There is a window on either side of the gateway. A pot with flowers is against one window and a cage with birds against the other.

Right, an upright piano; downstage a sewing-table and a couple of armchairs. Left of stage-centre is a desk or writing-table with a telegraph instrument on it. Below it, a whatnot with framed photographs, and close by, a couch. Against the wall, a sideboard. A lamp is hanging from the ceiling. On the wall, on either side of the piano, are two large laurel wreaths trimmed with ribbons. Between them is a portrait of a woman in stage costume. By the door is a hatstand with several swords and military equipment hanging from it. Nearby is a bureau and to the left, a barometer.

Scene One

It is a mild autumn evening. The gates of the fortress are open and a sentry is seen on the shore battery; he is wearing a busby with a brush. Now and then, his sword glitters in the red light of the setting sun. The sea is dark and calm.

THE CAPTAIN is sitting in the armchair, left, by the sewing-table. He is fumbling with a cigar that has gone out. He is in undress uniform, a bit threadbare, with riding boots and spurs. He looks tired and fed up. ALICE is sitting in the armchair on the right, doing nothing. She looks tired and apprehensive.

CAPTAIN
Why don't you play something?

ALICE
[*offhand but not crossly*] What shall I play?

CAPTAIN
Whatever you like.

ALICE
But you don't like my repertoire.

CAPTAIN
You don't like mine, either.

ALICE
[*evasively*] Do you want the doors left open?

CAPTAIN
Just as you like.

ALICE
We'll leave them then. Why aren't you smoking?

CAPTAIN
I'm beginning to find that strong tobacco doesn't agree with me.

ALICE

[*almost kindly*] Smoke something milder then. Smoking is your only pleasure, so you say.

CAPTAIN

Pleasure! What's that?

ALICE

Don't ask me. I know no more about it than you do. Don't you want your whisky yet?

CAPTAIN

I'll wait a little. . . . What's for supper?

ALICE

How should I know? Ask Kristin.

CAPTAIN

The mackerel ought to be in season. It's autumn, after all.

ALICE

Yes, it's autumn.

CAPTAIN

Inside and out. But apart from the autumn cold inside and out, a grilled mackerel with a slice of lemon and a glass of white Burgundy wouldn't be altogether out of place.

ALICE

You're getting quite eloquent.

CAPTAIN

Is there any Burgundy left in the wine cellar?

ALICE

To the best of my knowledge, we haven't had a wine cellar for the past five years.

CAPTAIN

You never know what we've got. Anyhow, we ought to lay in a store for our silver wedding. . . .

ALICE

You're not going to celebrate *that*, are you?

CAPTAIN

Of course I am.

ALICE

It would be more decent to hide our misery, all the twenty-five years of it. . . .

CAPTAIN

Alice, my dear, it *has* been misery, but we've had our fun, too. From time to time. You must make good use of the time that's left to you because when it's over, it's over!

ALICE
> Is it really over? I hope so.

CAPTAIN
> Yes, it's really over. What's left of us can be wheeled away on a barrow and dumped on the vegetable plot.

ALICE
> All that trouble for a plot in the garden.

CAPTAIN
> Yes, that's the way of the world; I didn't arrange it.

ALICE
> All that trouble! [*Pause.*] Has the postman been?

CAPTAIN
> Yes.

ALICE
> Was the butcher's bill there?

CAPTAIN
> Yes!

ALICE
> How much was it?

> > [THE CAPTAIN *takes a bill from his pocket, puts on his glasses and takes them off again.*]

CAPTAIN
> *You* look at it, will you? My sight's not so good.

ALICE
> What's the matter with your sight?

CAPTAIN
> I don't know.

ALICE
> Old age.

CAPTAIN
> Rubbish! I?

ALICE
> Well, certainly not I.

CAPTAIN
> Hm!

ALICE
> [*looking at the bill*] Can you pay it?

CAPTAIN
> Yes. But not immediately.

ALICE
> Later, I suppose. In a year's time, when you retire on a microscopic

pension! It'll be too late then, and when your illness comes back . . .

CAPTAIN

Illness? What illness? I've never been ill in my life. I was a bit seedy once, but that's all. I can go on for another twenty years!

ALICE

The Doctor had other ideas.

CAPTAIN

The Doctor!

ALICE

Who else could give a professional opinion about a disease?

CAPTAIN

I'm not ill. I've never been ill and I never will be ill. When I die, I'll just fall down dead on the spot like an old soldier!

ALICE

Talking about the Doctor, you know he's giving a party tonight.

CAPTAIN

[*worked up*] What of it? They haven't asked us because we won't have anything to do with them, and we won't have anything to do with them because we don't choose to. I find them contemptible. Riffraff! That's all they are! Scum!

ALICE

Everyone's scum according to you.

CAPTAIN

Everyone *is* scum.

ALICE

Except you!

CAPTAIN

Except me. Because I've always behaved decently, no matter what the circumstances. That's why I'm not scum.

[*Pause.*]

ALICE

Let's have a game of cards, shall we?

CAPTAIN

If you like.

ALICE

[*taking a pack of cards from the drawer in the sewing-table and shuffling them*] Would you believe it . . . the Doctor's using the band for a private party!

CAPTAIN

[*angrily*] That's because he goes into town and licks the Colonel's boots. Licks his boots, that's what he does! If you can do that . . . well!

ALICE

[*dealing*] I used to be quite friendly with Gerda, but she took advantage of me. . . .

CAPTAIN

They'd all take advantage of you. What's trumps?

ALICE

Put your glasses on.

CAPTAIN

They're no good. Well?

ALICE

Spades.

CAPTAIN

[*disappointed*] Spades?

ALICE

[*playing*] Well, you may be right. All the same, the new officers' wives have ignored us completely.

CAPTAIN

[*playing and taking the trick*] Who cares? We never give parties here so no one will notice. I can live with myself. . . . I always have.

ALICE

Me too! But Judith! She's growing up without any friends.

CAPTAIN

She'll have to find her own friends. . . . That was mine! Have you got any trumps left?

ALICE

One! Here, that's mine!

CAPTAIN

Six and eight make fifteen. . . .

ALICE

Fourteen! Fourteen!

CAPTAIN

Six and eight makes me fourteen. . . . I've forgotten how to count. And two makes sixteen . . . [*yawns*]. Your deal!

ALICE

You're tired.

CAPTAIN

[*dealing*] Not me!

ALICE

[*her ear cocked to open door*] You can hear the music all this distance. [*Pause.*] Do you think they've asked Kurt?

CAPTAIN
He arrived this morning, so he's had time to unpack his tails, even if he hasn't had time to call on us.

ALICE
Quarantine Officer? Is there going to be a Quarantine Station here?

CAPTAIN
Yes!

ALICE
He's my cousin, after all. We have the same family name. . . .

CAPTAIN
That's nothing to boast about. . . .

ALICE
[*sharply*] Now look here, leave my family out of this and I'll do the same for yours.

CAPTAIN
All right, all right, don't let's start that again.

ALICE
Is the Quarantine Officer a medical man?

CAPTAIN
No, he's a sort of clerk . . . an executive job. Kurt never had much of an education, did he?

ALICE
He never had any push, poor man.

CAPTAIN
He cost me a packet. . . . And when he deserted his wife and children . . . that put him beyond the pale.

ALICE
Not so hard on him, Edgar!

CAPTAIN
You know it's true. And what's he been doing in America since then? I can't say I'm pining to see him again! But he had his good points and I used to like to argue with him.

ALICE
Because he let you have it all your own way.

CAPTAIN
[*haughtily*] Own way or not, he was a person you could talk to. . . . There's not a soul on this island who understands me. They're all idiots. . . .

ALICE
It's strange, isn't it, that Kurt should get here just in time for our silver wedding . . . whether we celebrate it or not? . . .

CAPTAIN

What's strange about it? Oh, I see what you mean. . . . It was Kurt who brought us together, or married you off, or whatever they call it.

ALICE

Well, didn't he?

CAPTAIN

He certainly did! It was his idea! I leave you to say what a bright idea it was!

ALICE

A ridiculous idea . . .

CAPTAIN

And we've had to pay for it, not he.

ALICE

If only I'd stuck to the theatre. All my friends are stars now!

CAPTAIN

[*getting up*] Well, fancy that! I'll have my drink now! [*He goes to the sideboard and helps himself to a whisky and soda. He drinks, standing.*] There ought to be a footrail here, then we could imagine ourselves back in Copenhagen, in the American Bar.

ALICE

We'll have to put one in just to remind us of Copenhagen. They were the happiest days we had.

CAPTAIN

[*drinking greedily*] Yes. Do you remember Nimb's *navarin aux pommes?*

ALICE

No, but I remember the concerts at the Tivoli.

CAPTAIN

Your taste is so exquisite.

ALICE

You ought to be pleased to have a wife who is so cultured.

CAPTAIN

Oh, I am . . .

ALICE

When you need something to brag about. . . .

CAPTAIN

[*drinking*] They must be dancing at the Doctor's. . . . I can hear the bass tubas, three-four time, boom, boom, boom.

ALICE

It's the "Alcazar Waltz." I can hear the tune. It wasn't yesterday when I last danced a waltz.

CAPTAIN

Could you still manage it?

ALICE

Still?

CAPTAIN

Ye-es! Your dancing days are over. So are mine.

ALICE

I'm ten years younger than you!

CAPTAIN

That means we're the same age, doesn't it? The woman should always be ten years younger than the man.

ALICE

I like that! You're doddering. I'm in my prime.

CAPTAIN

Oh, I'm sure you can be charming to others—if you try hard enough.

ALICE

May we have the light on now?

CAPTAIN

By all means!

ALICE

Then ring!

> [THE CAPTAIN *goes to the desk, taking his time, and rings.* JENNY *enters, right.*]

CAPTAIN

Would you light the lamp, Jenny, please?

ALICE

[*sharply*] The hanging lamp!

JENNY

Yes, ma'am. [*Lights the hanging lamp while* THE CAPTAIN *watches her.*]

ALICE

[*curtly*] Have you cleaned the glass properly?

JENNY

Well enough.

ALICE

What kind of answer is that supposed to be?

CAPTAIN

Now, now, now . . .

ALICE

[*to Jenny*] You may go. I'll light the lamp myself. That will be the best thing.

JENNY
> I think so too! [*Goes to door.*]

ALICE
> [*getting up*] Go when I tell you.

JENNY
> [*hesitating*] I wonder what you'd say if I *did* go, ma'am. [ALICE *does not answer.* JENNY *goes out.*]

ALICE
> [*anxiously*] Do you think she'll walk out?

CAPTAIN
> [*going forward and lighting the lamp*] Wouldn't surprise me. And then we'll be in a nice mess. . . .

ALICE
> It's your fault. You spoil them!

CAPTAIN
> Don't be ridiculous. If you used your ears you'd know that they're always polite to me.

ALICE
> Because you kowtow to them! You're always kowtowing to people who don't matter. You're a dictator with the disposition of a slave.

CAPTAIN
> Bilge!

ALICE
> You kowtow to your men and your N.C.O.'s but you fall foul of your equals and superiors.

CAPTAIN
> Balderdash!

ALICE
> That's the way all tyrants behave! Do you think she'll leave?

CAPTAIN
> Yes, unless you go out and pacify her.

ALICE
> Me?

CAPTAIN
> If *I* go out you'll say I went there to flirt with the maids.

ALICE
> Suppose she goes. I'll have to do all the housework like last time. I'll ruin my hands!

CAPTAIN
> It'll be worse than that. If Jenny goes, Kristin goes too, and we'll never get another servant on the island again. The mate on the steamer

frightens away all the girls who come to us for a job . . . and if he doesn't, then my orderlies do it for him.

ALICE

Yes, your orderlies who come and gorge themselves in my kitchen because you're afraid to show them the door.

CAPTAIN

If I showed them the door, they'd never sign on for another term and the gun shop would have to close down.

ALICE

It would ruin us.

CAPTAIN

That's why the officers here are going to ask the King for a subsistence allowance.

ALICE

Who for?

CAPTAIN

For the orderlies.

ALICE

[*laughing*] You're crazy!

CAPTAIN

Yes, laugh! I can do with it.

ALICE

I'll have forgotten how to laugh soon. . . .

CAPTAIN

[*lighting his cigar*] That's something you must never forget. . . . It's miserable enough here, in all conscience.

ALICE

Well, let's say it's not very amusing. D'you want to go on playing?

CAPTAIN

No, it tires me out.

> [*Pause.*]

ALICE

I'm upset that the new Quarantine Officer should pay his first call here on people who are our enemies. He's my cousin after all.

CAPTAIN

There's no point in harping on it.

ALICE

Did you see the "Arrivals Column" in the paper? He was described as of independent means. He must have come into money, somehow.

CAPTAIN

Independent means, eh? A rich relative; he must be the first one in this family!

ALICE

In your family, I daresay. In mine we've had lots of rich people.

CAPTAIN

If he's come into money, it'll have gone to his head, but I'll soon put him in his place. And I'll see to it that he gets to know nothing about *my* affairs!

[*The telegraph is tapping.*]

ALICE

Who's that, I wonder?

CAPTAIN

[*staying where he is*] Quiet!

ALICE

Well, go and see then!

CAPTAIN

I can hear from here. I can hear what she's saying! It's Judith! [*Goes to the telegraph and taps out an answer; the apparatus goes on for a while and then* THE CAPTAIN *answers.*]

ALICE

Well?

CAPTAIN

Just a moment. [*Taps out his final answer.*] It was Judith. She's down at the guardhouse in town. She's a bit out-of-sorts again. She's staying away from school.

ALICE

Again! What else did she talk about?

CAPTAIN

Money, of course!

ALICE

Why is Judith in such a hurry? She needn't take her exams till next year.

CAPTAIN

Tell her that and see what good it does.

ALICE

You ought to tell her.

CAPTAIN

Haven't I told her over and over again? It's time you knew that children have wills of their own.

ALICE

They have in this house, anyway. [CAPTAIN *yawns.*] Must you yawn like that in your wife's face?

CAPTAIN

What else can I do? Day after day our conversation goes through the same routine. Haven't you noticed it? When you lashed out just now with your good old standby: "Here in this house, anyway," my counter should have been "It's your house as much as mine." But as I've already hit back a good five hundred times with that one, I yawned instead. My yawn could be construed to mean "You're absolutely right, my angel," or "Let's drop the subject," or it might have meant that I simply couldn't be bothered to reply.

ALICE

You're quite charming tonight.

CAPTAIN

Isn't it getting on for suppertime?

ALICE

Did you know the Doctor's ordered supper from the Grand Hotel for his party?

CAPTAIN

No. That means they're having ptarmigan. [*Succulently.*] Ptarmigan is the most delectable bird in the world, but it's sheer barbarism to roast it in pork fat.

ALICE

Ugh! Don't talk about food.

CAPTAIN

Wines then? I wonder what those barbarians are drinking with their ptarmigan?

ALICE

Do you want me to play for you?

CAPTAIN

[*sitting at the writing-table*] The last resort! Yes, but none of your funeral marches or hymns for the dead . . . they sound like music with a message. And I always want to join in with "Oh, misery me! Miaow, miaow!" "Now you know what a terrible husband I've got! Groan, moan, groan! If only he'd hurry up and die!" A jubilant roll of drums, fanfares, the final bars of the "Alcazar Waltz"! The "Champagne Galop"! Talking of champagne, I think we still have a couple of bottles left. Let's bring them up and pretend we have company.

ALICE

Certainly not. They're mine. They were a present to me.

CAPTAIN

You're always so close-fisted.

ALICE

And you're always downright stingy—to your wife, anyway.

CAPTAIN

Well, I'm lost for ideas. Shall I do a jig for you?

ALICE

No thank you! I've told you your dancing days are over.

CAPTAIN

You ought to invite a friend, a woman, to stay with you.

ALICE

Thank you! You ought to have a friend, a man, to stay with you.

CAPTAIN

Thank you! That's been tried to our mutual dissatisfaction. But it was interesting as an experiment. The moment the stranger came in we brightened up considerably . . . to start with . . .

ALICE

And then . . .

CAPTAIN

Oh, let's drop the subject!
        [*There is a knock on the door, left.*]

ALICE

Who can that be so late?

CAPTAIN

Jenny isn't in the habit of knocking.

ALICE

Go and open the door, and don't shout "come in." It makes the place like a workshop!

CAPTAIN

[*going towards the door, left*] Workshops aren't in your line.
        [*Another knock.*]

ALICE

Open it!

CAPTAIN

[*opening door and taking the visiting card that is handed in*] It's Kristin. Has Jenny left? [*The answer cannot be heard by the audience; to* ALICE:] Jenny's left us!

ALICE

So I'm a maid-of-all-work again!

CAPTAIN

And I'm the gentleman's gentleman!

ALICE

Can't you get one of your men to help in the kitchen?

CAPTAIN

Not these days.

ALICE

But it couldn't have been Jenny who sent in that card?

CAPTAIN

[*looking at the card with his glasses on, then handing it over to* ALICE] You read it. I can't see.

ALICE

[*reading the card*] Kurt! It's Kurt. Hurry out and bring him in.

CAPTAIN

[*going out, left*] Kurt! Well, well, this is a pleasure!

[ALICE *arranges her hair and seems to come to life.*]

CAPTAIN

[*entering left, with* KURT] Here he is, the son-of-a-gun. Welcome, old man! Give us your fist!

ALICE

[*to* KURT] Welcome to my home, Kurt.

KURT

Thank you. It's been such a long time!

CAPTAIN

How long is it? Fifteen years! And we've grown old. . . .

ALICE

Kurt looks exactly the same to me.

CAPTAIN

Sit down, please sit down! First of all, what are your plans? What are you doing this evening?

KURT

I've been invited to the Doctor's, but I haven't promised to go.

ALICE

Then stay here with us.

KURT

That would be the natural thing to do, but the Doctor's my chief and he'll take it out of me later.

CAPTAIN

What nonsense! I've never been afraid of my superiors. . . .

KURT

Afraid or not, there's certain to be trouble.

CAPTAIN

On this island, I'm the master. Keep behind me, and nobody will dare lay a finger on you.

ALICE

Be quiet, Edgar! [*Taking* KURT's *hand.*] Forget all about masters and superiors and stay with us. It's right and proper that you should.

KURT

If you say so! Especially as I feel so at home here.

CAPTAIN

Why shouldn't you feel at home. . . . There are no hard feelings, are there? [KURT *cannot hide a certain embarrassment.*] Why should there be? You were a bit wild, but you were young. It's all over and done with, as far as I'm concerned. I never bear malice.
[ALICE *looks annoyed. They are all sitting at the sewing table.*]

ALICE

Well, you've seen something of the world, haven't you?

KURT

Yes, and now I've landed on you . . .

CAPTAIN

. . . whom you married off to me twenty-five years ago.

KURT

Well, that's not the way it was, but it doesn't matter. It's nice to see that you're still together after twenty-five years. . . .

CAPTAIN

Yes, we've stuck it out. It hasn't always been a bed of roses, but as you said, we're still together. And Alice has nothing to complain about; lots to do and lots of cash! I don't suppose you know I'm a famous author. I write textbooks. . . .

KURT

Yes, I remember you published a book on "Firearms And How To Use Them" just before we parted. It was doing very well. Is it still a standard work?

CAPTAIN

It's still in use and it's still the most popular one of its kind, though they've tried to push it out for someone else's tinpot effort. . . . Absolutely useless, but in use, too, I'm afraid!
[*A painful silence.*]

KURT

You've been abroad, I hear.

ALICE

Would you believe it, we've been to Copenhagen five times?

CAPTAIN

Well, when I took Alice away from the theatre . . .

ALICE
>   Oh, you took me, did you?

CAPTAIN
>   Yes, I took you as a wife should be taken. . . .

ALICE
>   Oh, you're so gallant!

CAPTAIN
>   But since it was always being thrown in my face that I ruined her scintillating career . . . hm . . . I had to make it up to her by promising to take her to Copenhagen. . . . I've kept my promise so faithfully that we've been there five times! Five! [*Holds up the five fingers of his left hand.*] Have you been to Copenhagen?

KURT
>   [*smiling*] No, I've been to America mostly. . . .

CAPTAIN
>   America? Crude sort of place, isn't it?

KURT
>   [*surprised*] Well, it's not *Copenhagen!*

ALICE
>   Do you . . . hear . . . from your children?

KURT
>   No!

ALICE
>   You mustn't mind me saying this, Kurt, but it was rather inconsiderate of you to leave them like that. . . .

KURT
>   I didn't leave them. The court gave their mother custody. . . .

CAPTAIN
>   Don't let's talk about that now. In my opinion, it was a good thing for you that you got out of that mess!

KURT
>   [*to* ALICE] How are your children?

ALICE
>   They're well, thank you. Judith's at school in town.

CAPTAIN
>   They're very bright. The boy has a brilliant mind, brilliant. He could have got on to the General Staff. . . .

ALICE
>   He went abroad instead.

CAPTAIN
>   He had the makings of a Minister of War, too.

KURT

> Going off at a tangent . . . there's going to be a Quarantine Station here . . . the plague, cholera and so on. The Doctor will be my chief, as you know. . . . What sort of a man is he?

CAPTAIN

> Man? He's no man at all! Just an ignorant ape!

KURT

> [*to* ALICE] That's not going to make things easy for me.

ALICE

> It's not as bad as Edgar makes out, but I must confess that I can't take to him. . . .

CAPTAIN

> An ape, that's what he is! And the rest of them, too, the Customs Officer, the Postmaster, the telephone girl, the chemist, the pilot . . . the what-the-hell-do-they-call-him, the Alderman—apes, the lot of them. That's why I won't have anything to do with them!

KURT

> Aren't you speaking to any of them?

CAPTAIN

> Not to any of them!

ALICE

> It's true, they're people you just can't associate with.

CAPTAIN

> It's as if all the tyrants in the country had been exiled to this island.

ALICE

> [*ironically*] Exactly.

CAPTAIN

> [*good-naturedly*] Hm! Was that one at me? I'm no tyrant, not in my own house, anyway!

ALICE

> Mind your step, that's all!

CAPTAIN

> [*to Kurt*] You mustn't take her seriously. I'm a very understanding husband, and my old girl is the best wife in the world.

ALICE

> Would you like a drink, Kurt?

KURT

> Not now, thanks.

CAPTAIN

> Have you become . . .

KURT
  I drink in moderation.
CAPTAIN
  American habit?
KURT
  Must be.
CAPTAIN
  Drink like a fish or not at all. That's what I think! A man should be
  able to hold his liquor.
KURT
  Getting back to our neighbors on the island here—my job's going to
  bring me into contact with all of them—I don't suppose it'll be easy to
  steer a clear course. . . . You know how you get caught up in other
  people's affairs no matter how hard you try to keep out.
ALICE
  You'll have to get to know them but you'll come back to us because
  your real friends are here.
KURT
  Isn't it horrible to live here alone with enemies all round you?
ALICE
  I wouldn't say it's funny!
CAPTAIN
  There's nothing horrible about it! All my life I've had nothing but
  enemies, and they've helped me more than they've harmed me. And
  when I die, I'll be able to say that I owe nothing to anybody, that I've
  never got anything for nothing and that I've had to fight for every-
  thing I've got.
ALICE
  Edgar's path wasn't strewn with roses.
CAPTAIN
  Thorns and stones—flint—but a man has his own strength. Do you
  know what I mean?
KURT
  [*simply*] Yes, and it's not enough. I learnt that ten years ago.
CAPTAIN
  Then you're a weakling!
ALICE
  [*to* THE CAPTAIN] Edgar!
CAPTAIN
  Yes, he's a weakling if he can't fight for himself. Oh, I know that when
  the engine fails, all that's left is a barrowful to be dumped on a

garden plot, but as long as the engine's working, you have to hit out and kick out, hands and feet, for all you're worth. That's my philosophy.

KURT

[*smiling*] I enjoy listening to you. . . .

CAPTAIN

But you don't believe me?

KURT

No, I don't.

CAPTAIN

Well, it's true, all the same.

> [*The wind has been rising during the last scene. One of the doors in the background shuts with a clatter.*]

CAPTAIN

[*getting up*] A storm's blowing up. I feel it in my bones. [*He goes and shuts the door and taps the barometer.*]

ALICE

[*to Kurt*] You'll stay for supper, won't you?

KURT

Yes, thank you!

ALICE

It'll be very simple. Our maid has just walked out!

KURT

I'm sure it will be very appetizing.

ALICE

You're so easily satisfied, Kurt, my dear.

CAPTAIN

[*at the barometer*] You should see the way the barometer's falling! I told you it was coming.

ALICE

[*to* KURT, *whispering*] He's nervous!

CAPTAIN

What about that supper?

ALICE

[*getting up*] I'm going to see to it now. You two stay here and talk about life. . . . [*To* KURT, *whispering.*] Don't contradict him or he'll lose his temper. And don't ask why they never made him a major.

> [KURT *nods.* ALICE *starts out, right,* THE CAPTAIN *sits down at the sewing-table with* KURT.]

CAPTAIN

See that we have something nice to eat, old girl!

ALICE

Give me the money and you'll get it.

CAPTAIN

Always money! [ALICE *goes out. To* KURT.] Money, money, money! All day long, I have to keep my purse handy; I end up believing I *am* a purse. Do you know the feeling?

KURT

Yes, except that in my case, I believe I'm a pocketbook.

CAPTAIN

Ha ha! So you're onto them! These women! And you got hold of a real corker, you did!

KURT

[*patiently*] That's best forgotten now.

CAPTAIN

A real jewel! . . . As for me, I paired off with a nice woman; she's quite a good sort, in spite of everything.

KURT

[*smiling good-naturedly*] In spite of everything.

CAPTAIN

You needn't laugh!

KURT

[*as before*] In spite of everything.

CAPTAIN

Yes, she's been a faithful wife, an excellent mother, very excellent . . . but [*glancing at the door, right*] she's got the temper of a fiend. You know, there have been times when I've cursed you for palming her on to me.

KURT

[*good-naturedly*] But I didn't! Now, listen to me, my friend . . .

CAPTAIN

Now, now, now. You're talking nonsense and forgetting things you find it uncomfortable to remember! Don't take offense. You see, I'm used to giving orders and laying down the law, but you know me, so don't get riled.

KURT

I'm not the least bit riled. But I never foisted your wife on you. On the contrary . . .

CAPTAIN

[*not letting his flow of words be interrupted*] All the same, don't you think life is strange?

KURT

It certainly is.

CAPTAIN

And growing old . . . it might be interesting, but it's no joke! I'm anything but old, and yet, it's beginning to make itself felt. The people you know die off, and you get so lonely!

KURT

Happy the man who has a wife to grow old with him!

CAPTAIN

Happy? Yes, that is happiness; because your children leave you, too, don't they? You shouldn't have left yours!

KURT

I didn't. They were taken away from me. . . .

CAPTAIN

Now don't get angry just because I say you shouldn't have . . .

KURT

But that's not what happened. . . .

CAPTAIN

Well, whatever happened, it's dead and buried now. But you *are* alone.

KURT

My dear Edgar, a person can get used to anything.

CAPTAIN

Can you . . . can you really get used to . . . to complete loneliness?

KURT

Well, look at me!

CAPTAIN

What have you done for yourself the last fifteen years?

KURT

What a question! The last fifteen years!

CAPTAIN

They say you've come into money, that you're a rich man.

KURT

I'm not.

CAPTAIN

I'm not going to borrow anything. . . .

KURT

If you were, I'd be ready. . . .

CAPTAIN

Thank you very much, but I've still got a bit in the bank—You see— [*Glances over to door, right.*] This house must lack for nothing. . . . The very day I ran out of money, she'd walk out on me!

KURT

Oh, surely not!

CAPTAIN

Oh yes she would! Would you believe it, she makes a special point of coming to me when I'm short of cash just for the pleasure of letting me know that I'm not providing for the family.

KURT

But I thought you said you had a large income.

CAPTAIN

I have got a large income . . . but it's not large enough.

KURT

Then it can't be large by normal standards. . . .

CAPTAIN

Life is strange, and so are we!
[*The telegraph begins to tap.*]

KURT

What's that?

CAPTAIN

Time signal.

KURT

Haven't you got a telephone?

CAPTAIN

Yes, in the kitchen, but we use the telegraph because the operators go around reporting everything we say.

KURT

Social life here must be impossible.

CAPTAIN

It's unbearable. But life itself is unbearable! And you—who believe in a sequel—do you think there'll be peace afterwards?

KURT

I think the storms and pitched battles will go on there, as well.

CAPTAIN

There, as well—if there is any there! I'd rather have complete annihilation!

KURT

Do you think annihilation will come without suffering?

CAPTAIN

I will drop down dead on the spot without any suffering.

KURT

So you know that, do you?

CAPTAIN

Yes, I do!

KURT

You're not satisfied with life as you know it, are you?

CAPTAIN

[*sighing*] Satisfied? I'll be satisfied the day I die!

KURT

[*rising*] You can't know that for certain. . . . But tell me, what are you up to in this house? What's going on here? Even the walls give out the smell of poison. I felt sick the moment I came in. If I hadn't promised Alice to stay, I'd be out of here like a shot. There are dead bodies under the floors; and so much hatred one can hardly breathe. [THE CAPTAIN *seems to have shrunk into himself and is staring into space.*] What's the matter? Edgar?

[THE CAPTAIN *does not move.*]

KURT

[*taking* THE CAPTAIN *by the shoulders and shaking him*] Edgar!

CAPTAIN

[*coming round*] Did you say anything? [*Looking round him.*] I thought it was Alice! . . . Oh, it's you?—Listen . . . [*Relapses into unconsciousness again.*]

KURT

This is terrible! [*Goes to door, right, opens it.*] Alice!

ALICE

[*entering, wearing an apron*] What's the matter?

KURT

I don't know! Look at him!

ALICE

[*calmly*] He goes off like that now and again. . . . I'll play something. It'll bring him round.

KURT

No, don't! That's not the way to do it. Leave it to me! Can he hear? Or see?

ALICE

At the moment—no.

KURT

And you can tell me that so calmly! . . . Alice, what's going on in this house!

ALICE

Ask him there!

KURT

Him there? But he's your husband!

ALICE

To me he's a stranger, as much of a stranger as he was twenty-five years ago! I know nothing about that man, except that . . .

KURT

Quiet! He may hear you!

ALICE

He can't hear anything now!

> [*A bugle call outside.* THE CAPTAIN *springs to his feet, and grabs his sword and cap.*]

CAPTAIN

Excuse me! Sentry inspection! [*Goes out through the doors, back.*]

KURT

The man's ill! What is it?

ALICE

I don't know!

KURT

Is he out of his mind?

ALICE

I don't know!

KURT

Or is it drink?

ALICE

He boasts about it more than he indulges.

KURT

Sit down and tell me about it; calmly now and keep to the facts.

ALICE

[*sitting down*] What can I tell you? That I've been shut up in this tower for a lifetime, guarded by a man I've always hated and whom I hate so much now that the day he dies, I'd laugh out loud.

KURT

Why didn't you leave him?

ALICE

God knows! We broke it off twice when we were engaged. Since then we've tried to part company every day of our lives . . . but we're chained together; we can't break away! Once we *did* part—here in this house— it went on for five years. Now, only death can part us; we know it, and we're waiting for him to liberate us.

KURT

But why are you so . . . isolated here?

ALICE

Because he's kept me isolated from everybody. To start with he got my brothers and sisters out of the house—it's his own phrase, "got them out"—then my friends and everyone else. . . .

KURT

But what about *his* relations? Did you get them out?

ALICE

Yes, because they were robbing me of my good name and trying to kill me with their slanders. The time came when that telegraph was my only way of keeping in contact with the world and with human beings—the telephone was being tapped by the operator. He doesn't know, but I've taught myself how to use it. You mustn't tell him. He'd kill me if he knew.

KURT

This is incredible! Incredible! But why does he blame *me* for your marriage? Let me tell you what happened. You know he was my friend when we were young men. He fell in love with you the first time he saw you. He came to me and asked me to put in a good word for him. I said no, at once. You see, my dear Alice, I knew how cruel you could be and how you liked to ride roughshod over everyone. That's why I warned him . . . but he went on and on, so I sent him to ask your brother to speak up for him.

ALICE

I believe that's what did happen; but he's been lying to himself about it all these years, and you'll never make him believe anything else now.

KURT

All right, let him blame me if it makes him feel any better.

ALICE

Really, that's too much. . . .

KURT

I'm used to it . . . but what does hurt me is his accusation that I abandoned my children. . . . It's so unjust. . . .

ALICE

He's like that; he says what suits him and then he believes it. But he seems to have taken to you, probably because you don't contradict him. . . . Try not to get tired of us. . . . I think you've come at the right moment; it must be an act of providence. . . . Kurt! You mustn't get bored with us, because we must be the most unhappy people in the whole world! [*She cries.*]

KURT

One marriage I've seen at close quarters . . . and that was horrible.

But this is almost worse!

ALICE

Do you think so?

KURT

Yes!

ALICE

Whose fault is is?

KURT

The moment you stop asking whose fault it is, you'll feel better. Try to accept it as a fact, as something you have to put up with. . . .

ALICE

I can't. It's too much! [*Getting up.*] It's hopeless!

KURT

I pity both of you! . . . Do you know *why* you hate each other?

ALICE

No, it's the most unreasoning hatred. There's no cause for it, and no purpose, but there's no end to it, either. And do you know why he fears death most? He's terrified I might marry again.

KURT

Then he loves you!

ALICE

Perhaps! But it doesn't stop him from hating me!

KURT

[*as if to himself*] It's what we call love-hate and it comes from the hell inside us. . . . He likes you to play to him, doesn't he?

ALICE

Yes, but only cheap melodies . . . that awful "Entry of the Boyars," for instance. Whenever he hears it, it goes to his head and he wants to start dancing.

KURT

Does he dance?

ALICE

Yes, he's very funny sometimes!

KURT

There's one thing . . . excuse my asking. Where are the children?

ALICE

I don't suppose you know, but two of them died.

KURT

So you've had to suffer that, too?

ALICE

What haven't I suffered?

KURT

But the other two?

ALICE

I told you. Judith's at school in town. The boy went abroad. They couldn't stay here! He set them against me. . . .

KURT

And you set them against him.

ALICE

Yes, of course. So they took sides, there were bribes, canvassing . . . in order not to destroy them, we sent them away. What should have been the link between us became the final break, what should have been a blessing in the home became a curse. . . . I feel sometimes that the whole family is under a curse!

KURT

Since the Fall, yes, that's true!

ALICE

[*with a venomous look and in a sharp voice*] What fall?

KURT

The Fall in the Garden of Eden.

ALICE

Oh, that? I thought you meant something else!
    [*Embarrassed silence.*]

ALICE

[*clasping her hands*] Kurt! My cousin, my friend since childhood! I haven't always behaved to you as I should! But I'm being punished, and you're having your revenge!

KURT

Not revenge! I don't believe in revenge! No more of that talk!

ALICE

Do you remember one Sunday, after your engagement, I had invited you to dinner. . . .

KURT

Never mind about that!

ALICE

I must speak! Take pity on me! . . . When you came to dinner, we were out and you had to go away again.

KURT

You'd been invited out yourselves; don't harp on it!

ALICE

When I asked you to stay for supper before, I thought there was something in the larder! [*Hides her face in her hands.*] The place is bare, not even a crust of bread! . . . [*She cries.*]

KURT

Poor, poor Alice!

ALICE

But when he comes back and wants something to eat, and there's nothing for him, then the fireworks will start. You've never seen him in a temper. . . . Oh God, it's so degrading!

KURT

Would you mind if I go out and get something?

ALICE

There's nothing you can get on this island!

KURT

Not for my sake, but for his and yours . . . let me think of something, something . . . we'll laugh it off when he comes back. . . . I'll suggest we have a drink, and meanwhile I'll hit on something. . . . Get him into a good humor, play for him—any rubbish. . . . Sit at the piano and be ready!

ALICE

Look at my hands, are they fit to touch a piano? I have to polish the brass and wipe the glasses, make the fires and do the rooms. . . .

KURT

You have two servants, haven't you?

ALICE

Show! That's all that is! Because he's an officer! . . . But the servants are always leaving, so sometimes—mostly—we have no help at all. How am I going to get away with this . . . this supper? Oh, I wish the house would catch fire!

KURT

Alice, be quiet! Be quiet!

ALICE

If the sea would only sweep in and carry us off!

KURT

Stop it, I won't listen to you!

ALICE

What will he say, what will he say. . . . Don't go, Kurt, please don't leave me!

KURT

My poor friend! I'm not going to leave you!

ALICE

Yes, but when you do go . . .

KURT

Has he ever hit you?

ALICE

Hit me? Oh no, I'd have left him then. He knew it, too. I've *some* pride left.

> [*Outside we hear the sentry's voice: "Stop! Who goes there?"* —*and the reply: "Friend."*]

KURT

[*getting up*] Is that him?

ALICE

[*frightened*] Yes, it's him!

> [*Pause.*]

KURT

What on earth are we going to do?

ALICE

I don't know, I don't know!

> [CAPTAIN *enters at back. He is quite gay.*]

CAPTAIN

That's that; now, I'm free! . . . Well, she's been able to moan and groan to her heart's content! Isn't she a picture of misery?

KURT

What's the weather like outside?

CAPTAIN

Gusty! . . . [*Facetiously, opening one of the doors slightly.*] Sir Blue-beard and the maiden in the tower! Out there strides the sentry, his sword drawn, keeping watch over the beautiful maiden. . . . Ah! Here come the brothers, but the sentry is ready. Look at him! One, two! That's a brave man! Look at him! Hey diddle, diddle, hey diddle, diddle! Let's do the sword dance. You must see it, Kurt!

KURT

No, let's have the "Entry of the Boyars" instead!

CAPTAIN

So you know it, do you? . . . Alice, in your kitchen pinny, play in tune, however tinny. Come, I said.

> [ALICE *goes to the piano reluctantly.*]

CAPTAIN

[*pinching her arm*] You've been saying nasty things about me!

ALICE

I?

> [KURT *turns away.* ALICE *plays the "Entry of the Boyars."*
> THE CAPTAIN *does some kind of Hungarian dance behind the*

*writing-table, clicking his spurs. He collapses on the floor,
without being seen by* KURT *who is looking the other way,
or* ALICE, *who goes on playing the music to the end.*]

ALICE

[*without turning round*] Again? [*Silence. She turns and sees* THE
CAPTAIN *lying unconscious, but hidden from the audience by the
writing-table.*]

ALICE

Oh God! [*She remains there, her arms across her bosom, and sighs
with gratitude and relief.* KURT *turns around and hurries over to* THE
CAPTAIN.]

KURT

What is it? What is it?

ALICE

[*very tense*] Is he dead?

KURT

I don't know! Give me a hand!

ALICE

[*not moving*] I can't touch him . . . is he dead?

KURT

No, he's breathing!

        [ALICE *sighs.* KURT *helps* THE CAPTAIN *to his feet and puts
him in a chair.*]

CAPTAIN

What happened? [*Silence.*] What happened?

KURT

You fell.

CAPTAIN

What was the matter?

KURT

You fell down. How are you now?

CAPTAIN

Me? There's nothing the matter with me. Not a thing! Why are you
staring at me like that?

KURT

You're ill!

CAPTAIN

Oh rubbish! Go on playing Alice. . . . Oh, it's back again! [*His head in
his hands.*]

ALICE

You see, you *are* ill!

CAPTAIN

Don't shout! I fainted, that was all.

KURT

We must call a doctor! I'll go and telephone! . . .

CAPTAIN

I don't want a doctor!

KURT

You must! If only for our sake; otherwise we'll be held responsible.

CAPTAIN

If he comes here, I'll kick him out! I'll kill him! . . . Oh, it's here again!
[*His head in his hands.*]

KURT

[*going to the door, right*] I'm going to telephone. [*Goes.*]

[ALICE *takes off her apron.*]

CAPTAIN

Will you give me a glass of water?

ALICE

I suppose I'll have to. [*She gives him a glass of water.*]

CAPTAIN

How gracious you are!

ALICE

Are you ill?

CAPTAIN

Forgive me for not being well.

ALICE

Are you going to look after yourself then?

CAPTAIN

I've an idea that you won't do it.

ALICE

You're absolutely right about that!

CAPTAIN

The time has come. You've been waiting a long time for it.

ALICE

Yes, and you thought it never *would* come!

CAPTAIN

Don't get annoyed with me!

KURT

[*coming in, right*] Really, it's quite disgusting. . . .

ALICE

What did he say?

KURT

Nothing. He rang off.

ALICE

[*to* THE CAPTAIN] That's what your unbelievable arrogance has done!

CAPTAIN

I think I'm getting worse! . . . Try to get a doctor from town!

ALICE

[*going to the telegraph*] I'll have to telegraph then!

CAPTAIN

[*half sitting up in surprise*] You—know—how to use it?

ALICE

[*telegraphing*] Yes.

CAPTAIN

Well, I never! . . . Go on then! . . . The treachery of the woman! [*To* KURT.] Come and sit beside me, will you? [KURT *sits down at* THE CAPTAIN'S *side.*] Hold my hand! I'm sitting here and yet I'm falling. Can you imagine that? Downwards somehow! It's a strange feeling!

KURT

Have you had any attacks like this before?

CAPTAIN

Never!

KURT

While you're waiting for an answer from town, I'll go round and see the Doctor. Has he ever attended you in the past?

CAPTAIN

Yes.

KURT

Then he knows your case. . . . [*Moves left.*]

ALICE

There'll be an answer here soon. It's very good of you, Kurt! But come back soon!

KURT

As soon as I can! [*Goes out.*]

CAPTAIN

Kurt is kind. And how he's changed!

ALICE

Yes, for the better! But I'm sorry he has to get himself embroiled in our misery just now.

CAPTAIN

It's lucky for us! . . . I wonder how his affairs are really going! Did you notice that he wouldn't talk about them?

ALICE

I did notice it, but, as far as I know, nobody asked him!

CAPTAIN

Think of it—his life! And ours! I wonder if the same sort of thing happens to everyone.

ALICE

Perhaps, but everyone doesn't talk about it, as we do!

CAPTAIN

Sometimes I think misery attracts misery, and that the happy ones of the world shun the unhappy. That's why we never see anything but the seamy side of life.

ALICE

Have you known anyone who's happy?

CAPTAIN

Let me think! . . . No! . . . Yes . . . the Ekmarks?

ALICE

I don't agree! You know she had that operation last year. . . .

CAPTAIN

That's true! Well then, I don't know. . . . Yes, the von Kraffts.

ALICE

Yes, they lived an idyllic life for a good fifty years, they were well-off, everyone looked up to them, the children were nice and they married well. Then along came the cousin; he committed that awful crime, went to prison and suffered the consequences—and that was the end of them. Their name was dragged through all the papers. . . . The Krafft murder made it impossible for any of that prominent family to be seen in public; even the children had to be taken away from their schools. . . . Good God!

CAPTAIN

I wonder what my trouble is.

ALICE

What do you think it is?

CAPTAIN

Heart or head! It feels as though my spirit wants to escape and go up in smoke.

ALICE

Have you got an appetite?

CAPTAIN

Yes! What about supper?

ALICE

[*crossing the stage anxiously*] I'll ask Jenny!

CAPTAIN

But she's left!

ALICE

Yes, of course she has!

CAPTAIN

Ring for Kristin; I want some fresh water!

ALICE

[*ringing*] If . . . [*Ringing again.*] She's not answering.

CAPTAIN

Go and see. She might have walked out, too!

[ALICE *goes and opens door, left.*]

ALICE

What's this? Her trunk is packed in the passage out here.

CAPTAIN

Then she *has* left!

ALICE

This is hell! [*She falls on her knees, her head on a chair, sobbing.*]

CAPTAIN

Everything happens at the same time. . . . And Kurt has to walk in and see the mess we're in! If anything else is going to happen to us, let it happen now, at once!

ALICE

Do you know what I think? Kurt's gone and won't be coming back!

CAPTAIN

I can well believe that of him!

ALICE

Yes, we've been cursed. . . .

CAPTAIN

What do you mean?

ALICE

Can't you see how everyone shuns us?

CAPTAIN

That doesn't worry me! [*The telegraph starts to tap.*] There's the answer! Ssh! I can hear it! . . . They've got no time! None of them! The liars! Scum!

ALICE

There you are, that's what you get for decrying your doctors . . . and never paying their bills!

CAPTAIN

That's not true. . .

ALICE

> Even when you could, you wouldn't pay them. You sneered at their
> work just as you sneered at everybody else's work, including mine. . . .
> They won't come! And the telephone's cut off, because you didn't
> regard that as worth anything, either. Nothing's worth anything to you
> except your guns and cannons!

CAPTAIN

> Don't stand there gabbling away. . . .

ALICE

> You cast your bread on the waters. . . .

CAPTAIN

> What sort of superstition is that? . . . You and your old wives' tales!

ALICE

> You'll see! . . . You know we owe Kristin six months' wages?

CAPTAIN

> She's pinched that much from us.

ALICE

> But I've had to borrow from her, too!

CAPTAIN

> That's not beyond you.

ALICE

> You're contemptible! You know I borrowed to pay for Judith's trip to
> town!

CAPTAIN

> Kurt's put up a fine show, I must say. [*Ironically.*] A scoundrel like
> the rest of them! And a coward! Hadn't the gumption to say he'd had
> enough of us and that the Doctor's party was more fun. I suppose he
> was expecting a rotten supper with us! . . . He's the same waster he
> always was!
>
> > [KURT *enters quickly, left.*]

KURT

> Well Edgar, this is the position. . . . The Doctor knows everything
> there is to know about your heart condition.

CAPTAIN

> My heart?

KURT

> Yes, you've had hardening of the arteries for quite a time.

CAPTAIN

> Hardening of the arteries?

KURT

> And . . .

CAPTAIN

Is it serious?

KURT

Yes, that is . . .

CAPTAIN

It *is* serious!

KURT

Yes!

CAPTAIN

Fatal?

KURT

You must be very careful! To start with: away with that cigar! [THE CAPTAIN *throws it away*.] Next: away with the whisky! . . . Next: to bed!

CAPTAIN

[*frightened*] No, not that! Not bed! That's the end! Once you're there, you're there for good. I'll sleep on the couch tonight. What else did he say?

KURT

He was very nice. He'll come at once if you want him!

CAPTAIN

He was nice, was he, the hypocrite? I don't want him! . . . May I eat anything?

KURT

Not tonight. And nothing but milk for the next few days.

CAPTAIN

Milk! It's enough to make me heave. . . .

KURT

You'll have to learn to like it.

CAPTAIN

I'm too old to learn. [*His head in his hands*.] Oh! It's back again! [*He remains seated, staring fixedly ahead*.]

ALICE

[*to* KURT] What did the Doctor say?

KURT

He might die!

ALICE

Thank God!

KURT

Careful, Alice! Careful! And now, bring a pillow and a blanket and I'll put him here on the couch. . . . I'll spend the night in the chair.

ALICE
  What about me?
KURT
  You go to bed. He gets worse when he looks at you.
ALICE
  Command and I'll obey. You mean well by both of us! [*Goes out, left.*]
KURT
  That's right, both of you. I'm not getting mixed up in your quarrels!
  [*Takes the water bottle and goes out, right.*]

> [*The wind is blowing hard outside; the door blows open and
> an old woman with a plain, unprepossessing face peers into
> the room.* THE CAPTAIN *wakes, sits up and looks around him.*]

CAPTAIN
  So they've left me—those scoundrels! [*Noticing the old woman and
  getting nervous.*] Who are you? What do you want?
OLD WOMAN
  I only wanted to close the door, sir.
CAPTAIN
  Why? Why?
OLD WOMAN
  Because it blew open as I was passing.
CAPTAIN
  You came here to steal, didn't you?
OLD WOMAN
  There's nothing much to steal here, judging by what Kristin told me.
CAPTAIN
  Kristin!
OLD WOMAN
  Good night, sir. Sleep well! [*She closes the door and leaves.*]
        [ALICE *enters, left, with pillows and a blanket.*]
CAPTAIN
  Who was that at the door? Was anybody there?
ALICE
  Yes, it was old Maja from the Infirmary. She was passing by.
CAPTAIN
  Are you sure?
ALICE
  Are you afraid?
CAPTAIN
  Me? Afraid? Of course not!

ALICE

As you don't want to go to bed, you can sleep here.

CAPTAIN

[*lying down on the couch*] I'll stay here. [*He tries to take* ALICE's *hand, but she pulls it away.* KURT *enters with the water bottle.*] Don't leave me, Kurt.

KURT

I'm staying up with you all night! Alice is going to bed.

CAPTAIN

Good night then, Alice!

ALICE

[*to* KURT] Good night, Kurt!

KURT

Good night!

> [ALICE *goes out, left.* KURT *moves a chair to the couch and sits in it.*]

KURT

Aren't you going to take your boots off?

CAPTAIN

No! A soldier must always be at the ready!

KURT

You're expecting a battle then?

CAPTAIN

You never know! [*Sitting up.*] Kurt! You're the only man I've ever taken into my confidence. Listen. . . . If I die tonight . . . take care of my children!

KURT

I will!

CAPTAIN

Thank you. I trust you!

KURT

I wonder why you trust me?

CAPTAIN

We've never really been friends, but that's because I don't believe in friendship; and our families were born enemies; it's always been war to the knife between them. . . .

KURT

And you can still trust me?

CAPTAIN

Yes, but I don't know why! [*Silence.*] Do you think I'm going to die?

KURT

You, like everyone else! You won't be an exception.

CAPTAIN

You sound bitter.

KURT

I daresay. . . . Are you afraid of death? The wheelbarrow and the garden plot?

CAPTAIN

Supposing it's not the end!

KURT

Many people believe that!

CAPTAIN

And afterwards?

KURT

One surprise after another, I presume.

CAPTAIN

But no one knows for certain do they?

KURT

No, that's just it. And that's why you must prepare for anything.

CAPTAIN

I'm sure you're not so childish as to believe in hell?

KURT

Don't you believe in it? You're right in it now.

CAPTAIN

Only metaphorically.

KURT

You've shown me your hell realistically enough. No figure of speech, poetical or otherwise, could make it clearer.
[*Silence.*]

CAPTAIN

If you knew the anguish I'm going through.

KURT

Physical anguish?

CAPTAIN

No, it's not physical!

KURT

Then it must be spiritual; there's no other alternative.
[*Pause.*]

CAPTAIN

[*sitting up*] I don't want to die!

KURT
Earlier on, you wanted annihilation.

CAPTAIN
Yes, if it's painless!

KURT
But it isn't, is it?

CAPTAIN
Is this annihilation, then?

KURT
The beginning of it!

CAPTAIN
Good night!

KURT
Good night!

Scene Two

Same as before, but the lamp is spluttering; a dull morning can be seen through the windows and the panes of the front doors; the sea is boisterous. The sentry is at his post as before. THE CAPTAIN *is asleep on the couch;* KURT *is sitting at his side, pale and worn by his sleepless night.*

ALICE

[*entering, left*] Is he asleep?

KURT

Yes, since sunrise, if we could have seen it.

ALICE

What sort of a night did he have?

KURT

He dozed on and off, but he *would* go on talking.

ALICE

About what?

KURT

Religion. He argues like a schoolboy with the conviction that he has solved the riddle of the universe. Finally, just before dawn, he discovered the immortality of the soul!

ALICE

For his own glory!

KURT

Quite! . . . He is, without exception, the most arrogant man I've ever come across. "*I am; so God is.*"

ALICE

So it really has dawned on you! Do you see those boots? If he'd had the chance he'd have trampled the earth flat with them. He has trampled down other people's fields and gardens with them. He has trampled on other people's toes with them . . . and on my head. You killer! Your bullet has got you at last!

KURT

He'd be funny if he weren't so tragic, and there are glimpses of greatness in his selfishness. Have you one single good word to say for him?

ALICE

[*sitting*] Yes! Only he mustn't hear it; one word of praise makes him burst with self-esteem.

KURT

He won't hear anything, he's had a dose of morphine!

ALICE

Well, he came from a poor home. There were lots of sisters and brothers, and Edgar had to support the whole family by giving lessons. His father was no good, and that's putting it mildly. It must be hard on a young man to have to give up all the pleasures of youth, and slave for a tribe of ungrateful brats whom he hasn't brought into the world. When I was a little girl and he was a young man, I'd see him in the winter when it was twenty-five below zero. He had no overcoat . . . his little sisters were wrapped up in woolen coats . . . it was wonderful of him and I admired him for it; but he was so ugly, I used to shudder. He's extremely ugly, isn't he?

KURT

Yes, and sometimes his ugliness has something vicious about it. I used to notice it particularly when we fell out; in his absence his image would get horribly magnified and distorted. . . . He literally haunted me.

ALICE

Think of *me*, then! . . . But his early years as an officer must have been a martyrdom. Oh, he was helped out now and then by people with money. He'll never admit it. Everything he could get he took as his due—and no thanks to anyone.

KURT

We were going to speak well of him, weren't we?

ALICE

We will—when he's dead! I've told you as much as I can remember, anyway.

KURT

Would you say he's malicious?

ALICE

Yes, and yet he can be kind, even sentimental. . . . As an enemy, he's unrelenting.

KURT

Why haven't they made him a major?

ALICE

You ought to see the reason yourself! They didn't want to make a senior officer out of a man who'd shown himself such a tyrant when he was a junior officer! But you must never let him think you know! He says himself that he never wanted to be a major. . . . Did he talk to you about the children?

KURT

Yes, he's longing for Judith to come back.

ALICE

I'm quite sure of that! Do you know what Judith is? In character, she's his image. He's trained her to plague me. Would you believe it, my own daughter . . . has struck me!

KURT

What!

ALICE

Ssh! He's moving! . . . If he heard . . . He's so crafty. . . .

KURT

He's waking up.

ALICE

Doesn't he look like a devil? I'm terrified of him!

> [*Silence.* THE CAPTAIN *stirs, wakes, sits up, and looks round.*]

CAPTAIN

It's morning, at last! . . .

KURT

How are you now?

CAPTAIN

Not so good.

KURT

Would you like a doctor?

CAPTAIN

No! . . . I want to see Judith.

KURT

Wouldn't it be sensible to set your affairs in order before—or in case—anything happens?

CAPTAIN

What do you mean? What *could* happen?

KURT

What happens to all of us.

CAPTAIN

You're driveling, man! You can take my word for it, I'm not dying yet. It's too soon to start rejoicing, Alice!

KURT

Think of your children! Make your will so that your wife can have the furniture, if nothing else.

CAPTAIN

Is she to get hold of my things while I'm still alive?

KURT

No! But if anything does happen, she shouldn't be thrown out on the street! She's cleaned, dusted and polished that furniture for the last twenty-five years, so she ought to have the right to keep it. Shall I send for the lawyer?

CAPTAIN

No!

KURT

You've got a heart like stone, worse even than I thought.

CAPTAIN

It's back again! [*He falls back, unconscious.*]

ALICE

[*going toward the right*] There's someone in the kitchen. I must see who it is.

KURT

Yes, do! There's not much you can do here.
                    [ALICE *goes out.*]

CAPTAIN

[*recovering consciousness*] Well, Kurt, how are you going to organize the Quarantine Station?

KURT

Oh, I'm sure it'll be all right!

CAPTAIN

I'm in charge on the island here, so you'll have to deal with me. Don't forget that!

KURT

Have you ever seen a Quarantine Station?

CAPTAIN

I? Before you were born! And I'll give you a piece of good advice;

don't site your disinfecting plant too close to the beach.

KURT

I was thinking I'd look for a place quite close to the sea. . . .

CAPTAIN

That shows how much you know about your job! Water is the natural home for germs; it's what they live in, isn't it?

KURT

But salt water destroys them!

CAPTAIN

Idiot! . . . Well, as soon as you've found somewhere to live, you'll be bringing your children to join you.

KURT

What makes you think they'll agree to be brought?

CAPTAIN

If you've got any guts, they will! It would make a good impression on the people round here to see you doing your duty in that matter . . .

KURT

I have always done my duty in that matter!

CAPTAIN

[*raising his voice*] . . . in that matter where you've behaved quite disgustingly. . . .

KURT

Haven't I told you . . .

CAPTAIN

[*continuing*] Because a man doesn't desert his children like that. . . .

KURT

Carry on, carry on!

CAPTAIN

I'm a relative of yours, an older relative too, so I feel it my duty to tell you straight, however unpalatable it might be . . . and you must take it in the right spirit. . . .

KURT

Would you like something to eat?

CAPTAIN

Yes, I would!

KURT

A light meal?

CAPTAIN

No, a solid meal!

KURT

That would finish you off altogether!

CAPTAIN

It's bad enough to be ill without having to starve, too!

KURT

That's the way things are!

CAPTAIN

And no drinking! And no smoking, either! Life isn't worth living!

KURT

Death demands sacrifices, otherwise he turns up before you know it.

ALICE

[*entering with several bunches of flowers, some telegrams and letters*] For you! [*Throws flowers on the desk.*]

CAPTAIN

[*flattered*] For me! . . . Let me see! . . .

ALICE

They're only from the N.C.O.'s, the gunners and the brass band.

CAPTAIN

You're jealous!

ALICE

Oh no! If they were laurel wreaths . . . that would be something different, but you'd never get them.

CAPTAIN

Hm! . . . Here's a telegram from the Colonel . . . read it, Kurt. The Colonel's a gentleman, after all . . . even though he *is* an idiot! . . . This is from . . . what does it say? It's from Judith! . . . Will you send her a telegram and ask her to come on the next steamer? . . . You see, I'm not without friends, after all! It's good of them to think of me when I'm sick. They know my qualities are much more than my rank; they know I'm a man without fear and without reproach.

ALICE

I'm trying to work this out! Are they congratulating you because you're ill?

CAPTAIN

You hyena!

ALICE

[*to* KURT] We used to have a doctor here. He was hated so much that after he left the island, they gave a dinner for him, in honour of his departure.

CAPTAIN

Put the flowers in vases. . . . I still think people are scoundrels and I'm not taken in by them, but, by God, these simple tributes are sincere . . . they couldn't be anything else!

ALICE

Fool!

KURT

[*reading a telegram*] Judith says she can't come; the steamer's held up by the gale.

CAPTAIN

Is that *all* she says?

KURT

No-o! . . . There's more.

CAPTAIN

Well?

KURT

She asks her father not to drink so much!

CAPTAIN

Impertinence! . . . Just like children! That's my only daughter! The apple of my eye . . . my Judith! My idol!

ALICE

And image!

CAPTAIN

That's life! And its supreme blessings! To hell . . . !

ALICE

You're reaping what you've sown! You set her against her mother, and she's turned against her father! And now tell me there's no God!

CAPTAIN

[*to* KURT] What does the Colonel say?

KURT

He grants you leave of absence.

CAPTAIN

Leave of absence? I didn't ask for it!

ALICE

I asked for it!

CAPTAIN

I won't take it!

ALICE

The order's gone out already.

CAPTAIN

That's nothing to do with me.

ALICE

You see, Kurt, for this man there are no laws, no statutes, no rules. . . . He's above everything and everybody; the universe was created for him and him alone, the sun and the moon go on their way to sing his praises to the stars; that's him, my husband . . . ! The insignificant Captain, who couldn't even reach the rank of Major, who thinks he's a figure of awe and whose bombast sets everyone sniggering behind his back. There he is, this frightened little man who cowers in the dark and pins his faith to barometers, and what will the end of the act be . . . a barrowful of manure, and poor quality manure at that!

CAPTAIN

[*fanning himself contentedly with a bunch of flowers, not listening to* ALICE] Have you asked Kurt to breakfast?

ALICE

No!

CAPTAIN

Then go and get us two nice juicy steaks at once—Châteaubriands.

ALICE

Two?

CAPTAIN

Yes. *I'm* going to have one.

ALICE

There are three of us here!

CAPTAIN

Are you having one as well? All right, get three then!

ALICE

And where am I going to get them? Last night, you asked Kurt to supper and there wasn't even a crust of bread in the house. Kurt's had to sit up all night on an empty stomach; he hasn't even had a cup of coffee because we haven't got any . . . and we haven't got any credit, either.

CAPTAIN

She's annoyed with me because I didn't die yesterday!

ALICE

No, because you didn't die twenty-five years ago, because you didn't die before I was born!

CAPTAIN

[*to* KURT] Listen to her! . . . This is what happens when you try your hand at matchmaking, Kurt! It's obvious enough that this marriage wasn't made in heaven!

> [ALICE *and* KURT *exchange meaning glances.* THE CAPTAIN *gets up and goes to the door.*]

CAPTAIN

Anyway, you can say what you like, I'm going on duty! [*He puts on an old-fashioned brush-helmet, his sword and his cape.* ALICE *and* KURT *try to stop him—in vain.*]

CAPTAIN

Out of my way! [*Goes out.*]

ALICE

Go, that's right! You always do; turn your back when the fight gets too hot for you, and then let your wife cover your retreat! You prize-drunkard, you! You braggart! You liar! To hell with you!

KURT

This really is hell!

ALICE

But you don't know everything yet!

KURT

What, is there more?

ALICE

I'm too ashamed. . . .

KURT

Where is he off to now? And where does his strength come from?

ALICE

That's the question! He's going to the Sergeants' Mess to thank them for the flowers . . . then they'll eat and have drinks all round. Then he'll run down the other officers. . . . If you knew how many times they've threatened to have him cashiered! It's only their pity for his family that has kept him his job! And he really fancies they're afraid of him because he's so much better than they are! As for those poor officers' wives who have put in a good word for us, he just hates them and slanders them.

KURT

I must confess that I came here to try and get some peace and quiet by the sea. . . . About your circumstances I knew nothing. . . .

ALICE

Poor Kurt! . . . Now, how can we scrape up a meal for you?

KURT

Oh, I'll go round to the Doctor's; but how about you? Let me arrange something for you.

ALICE

All right, but he mustn't hear about it. He'd kill me!

KURT

[*looking out of the window*] Look, he's out there on the rampart, right in the face of the gale!

ALICE

I'm sorry for him . . . because he's what he is!

KURT

I'm sorry for both of you! But what can we do about it?

ALICE

I don't know. . . . A whole bundle of bills came in, too. He didn't see them. . . .

KURT

It may be wise not to see things sometimes!

ALICE

[*at the window*] He's flung open his cape. He's bared his breast to the wind. He must want to die!

KURT

Not he! Just before, when he felt his life was running out, he made a grab at mine, and started managing my affairs as though he wanted to take possession of me and live my life.

ALICE

That's the vampire in him . . . to meddle in other people's destinies, to suck interest out of other people's lives, to arrange everything and settle everything for others; his own life is completely without interest for him. Remember that, Kurt, and don't let him inveigle himself into your family life, don't let him meet your friends, because he'll take them away from you and make them his own. . . . He's a real magician at that sort of thing! . . . If he ever met your children, they'd be his best friends in no time; he'd be their mentor and he'd educate them as he thinks fit, but before anything, against your wishes.

KURT

Alice! It wasn't he who took my children away from me at the time of the divorce, was it?

ALICE

Since it's over now; yes, it was he!

KURT

I suspected it, but never knew for certain! So it was he!

ALICE

You had so much trust in my husband that you sent him to act as peace-maker between you and your wife; well, he started making up to her instead, and told her how she could get custody of the children.

KURT

Oh God! . . . Oh God in heaven!

ALICE

So you've learned even more about him.
        [*Silence.*]

KURT

And only last night . . . when he thought he was dying . . . he made me promise to look after *his* children!

ALICE

But you wouldn't take revenge on *my* children, would you?

KURT

By keeping my promise? Yes, I'll look after your children!

ALICE

That's really the worst revenge you could take, because there's nothing he detests more than magnanimity!

KURT

So I may consider myself revenged! Without taking revenge!

ALICE

I love revenge when it's justice; it gives me a thrill to see how evil gets its deserts.

KURT

So that's still your view!

ALICE

It will always be my view. The day I forgave or loved an enemy, I'd be a hypocrite!

KURT

Alice, it can be a duty to turn a deaf ear or a blind eye. Magnanimity is a quality we can all do with.

ALICE

Not I! My life has always been open and straightforward. I have nothing to hide.

KURT

That's saying a lot.

ALICE

But not enough! What I have suffered, in all innocence, for the sake of this man, whom I never loved. . . .

KURT

Why did you marry him?

ALICE

Perhaps you can tell me . . . ! Because he took me! Seduced me! I don't know! I wanted to get on. . . .

KURT

By giving up your career?

ALICE

It was looked down on, anyway. But he tricked me! He held out prospects of a life of ease—a beautiful home; and all he had was debts . . . the only gold I saw was on his uniform, and that wasn't real. He tricked me!

KURT

Just a moment! When a young man falls in love, the future always looks rosy, doesn't it? If his hopes don't always materialize, you mustn't blame him. I ought to have it on my conscience, too, that my hopes miscarried, but I don't regard myself as a trickster! . . . What are you staring at on the rampart?

ALICE

I'm looking to see if he's collapsed again.

KURT

Has he?

ALICE

No, unfortunately! He's still tricking me!

KURT

Then I'll go round to the Doctor and the solicitor.

ALICE

[*sitting down by the window*] Yes, do go, Kurt. I'll stay here and wait. I have learnt how to wait!

Scene Three

The same scene. Daylight. The sentry is at his post on the battery, as before. ALICE *is sitting in the armchair, right; her hair has turned grey.* KURT *enters, left, after knocking at the door.*

KURT

Good morning, Alice!

ALICE

Good morning, my friend! Take a seat!

KURT

[*sitting down in the easy chair*] The steamer's just coming in.

ALICE

Then I know what to expect, if he's on board!

KURT

He is. I caught the glitter of his helmet. What's he been up to in town?

ALICE

I can work it out. He put on his parade dress, so he must have gone to see the Colonel; he took his best gloves with him, so he must have paid some calls.

KURT

Did you notice how subdued he was yesterday? Since he's stopped drinking he's been a different man, calm, reserved, considerate. . . .

ALICE

I know. If that man had never taken to drink he would have been even more of a threat to his fellow men. It may be a piece of luck for every-one else that whisky turned him into a harmless mountebank.

KURT

The bottle brought him down all right. But have you noticed that since he learned he is going to die, he has taken on a dignity that has raised him up again? It may be that his new ideas on immortality have changed his outlook on life.

ALICE

Don't deceive yourself. He's thinking up some new piece of mischief. And don't believe a word that comes out of his mouth, because his lies are all thought out beforehand. He understands the art of intrigue better than anyone.

KURT

[*looking at* ALICE] Alice! What's happened? You've gone grey in the last two days.

ALICE

No, my friend, I've been grey for a long time; it's only that I haven't bothered to touch up my hair now that my husband is as good as dead! Twenty-five years in a fortress. . . . Did you know that this was a prison in the old days?

KURT

A prison! The walls look like it!

ALICE

And my complexion! Even the children took on a prison colour when they were here!

KURT

I find it difficult to imagine little children prattling inside these walls.

ALICE

There wasn't much prattling here. And the two who died . . . they died from lack of light!

KURT

What do you think is going to happen now?

ALICE

The final onslaught on *us*. I saw a familiar glint in his eye when you read that telegram from Judith. It should, of course, have been aimed at her, but she's a privileged person, as you know, so his hatred struck at you.

KURT

What do you think he's got in store for me?

ALICE

Hard to say, but he has an uncanny gift for ferreting out other people's secrets. . . . Didn't you notice how he seemed to be living in your Quarantine Station all day yesterday, how he was working up an interest in life from your existence, and devouring your children alive? . . . The man-eater, you see! I know him. His own life is nearly over, or is over already. . . .

KURT

I've had that impression too—that he's on the other side already. His face has a sort of phosphorescence about it, as though he's started to decay . . . and his eyes glow like will-'o-the-wisps over graves or marshes. . . . Here he comes! Tell me, have you thought he might be . . . jealous?

ALICE

No, he's too conceited for that! "Show me the man I need to be jealous of!" They're his very words!

KURT

That's all to the good. Even his vices have their own virtue. Anyway, shall I go and greet him?

ALICE

No. Be offhand, or he'll think you're trying to take him in. And when he starts lying, let him think you believe him. I can decipher his lies all right; I can always discover the truth with my cryptogram. . . . Something terrible is about to happen, I feel it . . . but Kurt, don't lose your self-control! My only advantage in our long fight has been that I was always sober and consequently able to keep a grip on myself. He was always let down by his whisky! Now, we'll see!

> [THE CAPTAIN *enters, left, in parade dress, helmet, cape, white gloves. He is composed and dignified, but pale and hollow-eyed. His step is uncertain. He sits right of stage and some distance from* KURT *and* ALICE. *He is still wearing his cape and helmet. During the conversation that follows he keeps his sword between his knees.*]

CAPTAIN

Good morning! Excuse my sitting down like this, but I'm a bit tired.

ALICE *and* KURT

Good morning. Welcome back!

ALICE

How are you feeling?

CAPTAIN

Fine! A bit tired. . . .

ALICE

Any news from town?

CAPTAIN

Oh, bits and pieces of gossip. I saw the Doctor, among other things. He told me there was nothing much the matter with me, and that I could go on for another twenty years if I take care of myself.

ALICE

[*to* KURT] He's lying! [*To* THE CAPTAIN.] Well, I'm glad to hear that, my dear!

CAPTAIN

I am, too!

[*Silence during which* THE CAPTAIN *looks at* ALICE *and* KURT, *as though he is waiting for them to speak.*]

ALICE

[*to* KURT] Keep quiet. Let him do the talking. He'll soon give the game away.

CAPTAIN

[*to* ALICE] Did you say anything?

ALICE

No! Nothing!

CAPTAIN

[*slowly*] Listen, Kurt . . .

ALICE

[*to* KURT] Here it comes.

CAPTAIN

I . . . I've been in town, as you know.

[KURT *nods.*]

CAPTAIN

I . . . I made some new acquaintances . . . among others . . . a young cadet . . . [*hesitatingly*] in the Artillery! [*Pause, during which* KURT *shows some anxiety.*] We're below strength in cadets . . . so I arranged with the Colonel to have him posted here. It ought to please you, especially when I tell you that he . . . is . . . your own son.

ALICE

[*to* KURT] The vampire! There you are!

KURT

In normal circumstances, any father would be delighted. In my case, it is merely painful!

CAPTAIN

I don't see why.

KURT

You don't have to see why. It's enough that I don't want it!

CAPTAIN

Is it indeed . . . ! Then let me tell you that the young man will be reporting here and that, from then on, he's under my command.

KURT

Then I'll make him put in for a posting to another regiment!

CAPTAIN

You can't. You have no rights over your son!

KURT

Oh?

CAPTAIN

No. The court handed them over to his mother.

KURT

Then I'll get in touch with his mother!

CAPTAIN

You needn't bother.

KURT

Needn't bother?

CAPTAIN

No, because I've done so already. Well?

[KURT *gets up but sinks down again.*]

ALICE

[*to* KURT] Now he *must* die!

KURT

He *is* a man-eater!

CAPTAIN

So that's that! [*To* ALICE *and* KURT.] Did you say anything?

ALICE

No. Are you getting deaf?

CAPTAIN

Yes, a bit. . . . But if you come closer, I'll tell you something that's for your ears only.

ALICE

There's no need. And a witness could be useful to both parties, couldn't he!

CAPTAIN

You're right. It's always useful to have a witness. But, first of all, did you get that will?

ALICE

[*handing him a document*] The solicitor drew it up himself.

CAPTAIN

In your favour! . . . Good! [*Reads the document, then tears it carefully into strips and throws them on the floor.*] And that's that!

ALICE

[*to* KURT] Have you ever seen a man like him!

KURT

He's not a man!

CAPTAIN

Well, Alice, I wanted to tell you this. . . .

ALICE

    [*anxiously*] Go ahead!

CAPTAIN

    [*calmly, as before*] In view of your desire, reiterated over a lengthy period, to put an end to the misery of this ill-assorted marriage; in view of your lack of feeling for your husband and children, and in view of your unwillingness to carry out your domestic duties, I took the opportunity while I was in town, of filing a petition for divorce in the County Court!

ALICE

    Really? And the grounds?

CAPTAIN

    [*calmly as before*] Besides the grounds I have just enumerated, there are others, purely personal ones. Now that I know I might live another twenty years, I am thinking of changing my unhappy married state for one that suits me better. I need a more congenial mate, someone who can show some devotion to her husband and who can bring into the home, not merely youth, but—let us be frank—a little beauty, too.

ALICE

    [*taking off her ring and throwing it at* THE CAPTAIN] There you are!

CAPTAIN

    [*picking up the ring and putting it into his waistcoat pocket*] She's flung her wedding ring away! Will the witness please take notice!

ALICE

    [*getting up, agitated*] You intend to turn me out and put another woman in my house?

CAPTAIN

    What if I do?

ALICE

    All right, then, we'll have a few home truths. . . . Kurt, I want you to know that this man tried to murder me.

KURT

    Murder?

ALICE

    Yes, he threw me in the sea!

CAPTAIN

    There were no witnesses!

ALICE

    He's lying! Judith saw it happen.

CAPTAIN

    Supposing she did?

ALICE

She can give evidence!

CAPTAIN

No, she can't. She says she saw nothing!

ALICE

You've taught the girl to lie!

CAPTAIN

I didn't have to; you'd done it already.

ALICE

You've been to see her?

CAPTAIN

Oh, yes. . . .

ALICE

My God! My God!

CAPTAIN

The fortress has surrendered! The enemy is given ten minutes to get out. [*Putting his watch on the table.*] Ten minutes by that watch on the table! [*Remains standing, his hand on his heart.*]

ALICE

[*going to* THE CAPTAIN *and pulling at his arm*] What's the matter?

CAPTAIN

I don't know!

ALICE

Would you like something, something to drink?

CAPTAIN

Whisky? No, I don't want to die! You . . . [*Straightening himself up.*] Don't touch me! . . . Ten minutes, or the garrison will be massacred! [*Draws his sword.*] Ten minutes! [*Exits, back.*]

KURT

What sort of man is this?

ALICE

He's a devil, not a man.

KURT

What does he want with my son?

ALICE

He wants him as a hostage so that he can trample on you. He wants to keep you away from the authorities on the island. . . . Do you know that the people here call this island "Little Hell"?

KURT

I didn't know! . . . Alice, you are the first woman for whom I've ever felt any pity. All the others, it seemed to me, got their deserts.

ALICE

Don't forsake me now! Don't leave me; he beats me. . . . He's been beating me for twenty-five years . . . in front of the children, too. . . . He threw me in the sea. . . .

KURT

That settles it. The man is my enemy. When I came here I had no rancour . . . the slanders, the humiliations, I'd forgotten them. I even forgave him when you told me that he was the man who had separated me from my children. . . . He was a sick man and I thought he was dying . . . but now, when he wants to steal my son from me, he must die . . . it's he or I.

ALICE

Good! Don't surrender the fortress! Blow it up, instead, and him, too, even if we have to die with him! I'll take charge of the gunpowder!

KURT

When I came here there was no bitterness in me. When I felt your hatred contaminating me, I thought of running away, but now I feel I must hate this man as I hate everything evil. . . . What can we do?

ALICE

He taught me the tactics! Get his enemies together and look for allies!

KURT

Think of it! He managed to seek out my wife! Why didn't those two meet a generation ago? There would have been battles to set the whole earth trembling!

ALICE

But now those twin souls have met . . . and they must part! I think I know his most vulnerable spot; I've suspected it for a long time. . . .

KURT

Who's his worst enemy here?

ALICE

The Quartermaster.

KURT

Can we trust him?

ALICE

Yes. . . . And he knows what I . . . I know, too! He knows what the Sergeant-Major and the Captain have been up to!

KURT

What have they been up to? Do you mean . . .

ALICE

Swindling their men.

KURT

That's terrible! No, I don't want to meddle in that!

ALICE

Ha ha! So you can't knock your enemy out?

KURT

I could once, but not any more.

ALICE

Why?

KURT

Because I've discovered . . . that, in the end, justice will be done.

ALICE

What, wait for it? By then your son will have been taken away from you! Look at my grey hair . . . feel how thick it still is . . . feel it! He hopes to get married again, and then I'll be free—to do the same—I *am* free! And in ten minutes he'll be under arrest, down there, down there . . . [*stamps on the floor*] down there . . . and I'll be dancing over his head. I'll dance to the "Entry of the Boyars." [*Takes a few dance steps, arms akimbo.*] . . . Ha-ha-ha-ha! And I'll play the piano, so that he can hear! [*Bangs on the piano.*] Oh! The tower is opening its gates, and the sentry, with his drawn sword, won't be guarding me any more, but him. . . . Hey diddle, diddle! Him, him! He'll be guarding him!

[KURT *has been eyeing her hungrily.*]

KURT

Alice, are you a devil, too?

[ALICE *jumps on a chair and tears down the laurel wreaths.*]

ALICE

I'll take these when I go . . . the laurel leaves of victory! And the fluttering ribbons! A bit grimy, but eternally green! Like my youth! I'm not old, am I, Kurt?

KURT

[*with shining eyes*] You are a devil!

ALICE

In "Little Hell." Look, I'm going to titivate myself. [*Letting down her hair.*] In two minutes, I'll be dressed; in another two minutes I'll be with the Quartermaster . . . and then, sky-high with the fortress!

KURT

You *are* a devil!

ALICE

You used to say that when we were children. Do you remember, when we were so high and we got engaged? Ha ha! You were so shy. . . .

KURT

[*seriously*] Alice!

ALICE

Yes, you were! But it suited you. You know, there are free and easy
women who like shy men, and they say there are shy men who like
free and easy women! . . . You used to like me a little bit then, didn't
you?

KURT

Here, I don't know where I am now!

ALICE

You're with an actress, whose manners are free and easy, but who's a
very good sort, despite that. Well, I'm free now! Free, free! . . . Turn
round, and I'll change my blouse. [*She unbuttons her blouse.* KURT
*rushes forward, takes her in his arms, lifts her in the air and bites her
neck, so that she cries out. Then he drops her unceremoniously on the
couch and hurries out, left.*]

Scene Four

The same scene. Evening. The sentry on the battery can still be seen through the window, back. The laurel wreaths are hanging over the back of a chair. The pendant lamp has been lit. Soft music. THE CAP-TAIN, *pale and hollow-eyed, his hair grizzled, wearing a shabby undress uniform and riding boots, is sitting at the desk, playing patience. He is wearing glasses. The entr'acte music continues after the rise of the curtain until* ALICE *comes in later.*

THE CAPTAIN *goes on with his patience, but every now and then he starts involuntarily or looks up and listens. The patience does not seem to work out. He gathers up the cards irritably, takes them to the window, left, opens it and throws them out. He leaves the window open, rattling on its hinges. He crosses to the sideboard but is put out by the noise made by the window, and turns round to see what the trouble is. He takes three dark, square bottles of whisky from the side-board, scrutinizes them carefully—then throws them out of the win-dow. He takes out some boxes of cigars, smells one of them, then throws them out of the window. After that he takes off his glasses, wipes them and, having tested his eyesight with them, throws them out of the window. He stumbles against the furniture as if he can't see clearly, and lights the six candles of the candelabra on the bureau. He catches sight of the laurel wreaths, takes them towards the window, but turns back. He takes the cover from the piano, carefully wraps it round the wreaths, fastens the corners with pins from the writing-table and puts the bundle on a chair. He goes to the piano, bangs the keys with his fists, locks it and throws the key out of the window. Then he lights the candles on the piano, goes to the whatnot, takes his wife's portrait, looks at it, tears it to shreds and throws them on the floor.*

The windows rattle and he jumps nervously. After that he calms down, takes the portraits of his son and daughter, kisses them hastily and puts them in his vest pocket. He sweeps the other portraits on to the floor with his arm and makes a pile of them with his boot.

Then he sinks down at the desk, tired out, and puts his hand up to his heart. He lights the table lamp, sighs and stares in front of him as if haunted by nightmares. He gets up, goes to the bureau, lifts the lid, takes out a bundle of letters tied up with blue silk ribbon and throws it into the tiled stove. He closes the bureau.

The telegraph gives one single tap. THE CAPTAIN *starts in mortal fear, and remains standing and listening, his hand on his heart. Hearing no more from the telegraph, he cocks his ear towards the door, left. He goes over, opens it, takes a step inside and comes back, carrying a cat. He is stroking its back. He goes out, right. The music stops.*

ALICE enters back, dressed for going out, with hat and gloves. Her hair is black again. She looks round, surprised at the many lighted candles. KURT *enters, left, looking nervous.*

ALICE

It looks like Christmas Eve here!

KURT

Well?

ALICE

[*holding out her hand to be kissed*] Thank me! [KURT *kisses her hand reluctantly.*] Six witnesses, four as firm as a rock. The charge has been brought and the reply is coming here by telegraph—here, right inside the fortress!

KURT

Indeed!

ALICE

You should say "Thank you" instead of "Indeed"!

KURT

Why has he lit all these candles?

ALICE

Because he's afraid of the dark, of course! Look at the telegraph! Doesn't it look like the handle of a coffee mill? I grind, I grind, and the beans crunch—it's like having your teeth out. . . .

KURT

What's he been doing here?

ALICE

It looks as though he's going to move! He'll move all right—down there!

KURT

Alice, don't! It goes against the grain! He used to be my friend. He helped me more than once when I was in trouble. I'm sorry for him!

ALICE

And what about me? I've done no harm but I've had to sacrifice my career for that monster!

KURT

What about that career? Was it really so brilliant?

ALICE

[*livid*] What's that you're saying? Don't you know who I am, who I used to be?

KURT

Come now! Come now!

ALICE

You're beginning, too. . . . Already?

KURT

Already?

> [ALICE *throws her arms round* KURT's *neck and kisses him.
> He takes hold of her arms and bites her neck. She cries out.*]

ALICE

You're biting me.

KURT

[*beside himself*] Yes, I want to bite your throat and suck your blood like a lynx. You've roused the wild beast in me. For years I've been trying to kill it by atonement and self-restraint. When I came here I thought I was a bit better than you two, but now I'm the most debased! I've seen you now in all your disgusting nakedness, my passion has distorted my vision and I feel all the power of evil; what is ugly becomes beautiful, what is good becomes ugly and sickly! . . . Come here —I'll stifle you . . . with a kiss! [*He embraces her.*]

ALICE

[*showing her left hand*] Look at the mark of the chain you've broken! I was a slave and you've set me free!

KURT

But I'm going to chain you up again. . . .

ALICE

You?

KURT

Yes!

ALICE

I thought for a moment that you were . . .

KURT

Devout?

ALICE

Yes, you talked about the Fall of Man. . . .

KURT

Did I?

ALICE

And I thought you came here to preach. . . .

KURT

Did you? . . . In an hour's time we shall be in town! Then you'll see what I am. . . .

ALICE

We'll go to the theatre tonight. I want everyone to see us. If I run away, they'll all blame him. You do see that, don't you?

KURT

I'm beginning to. Prison isn't enough.

ALICE

No, it's not enough! He must be disgraced, too!

KURT

A topsy-turvy world. *You* do something shameful and *he* pays the piper!

ALICE

Well, if the world is so silly . . . !

KURT

It's as if these prison walls had been impregnated with all the sins of the criminals and you only have to breathe here to get infected yourself. You were thinking of the theatre and supper, weren't you? I was thinking of my son!

ALICE

[*striking him across the mouth with her glove*] Hypocrite!

[KURT *raises his hand to strike her.*]

ALICE

[*drawing back*] *Tout beau!*

KURT

Forgive me!

ALICE

On your knees, you! [*He kneels.*]

On your face! [*He touches the floor with his forehead.*]

Kiss my foot! [*He kisses her foot.*]

And never do that again! Now get up!

KURT

[*getting up*] How low have I sunk? Where am I?

ALICE

You know where you are!

KURT

[*looking round with horror*] I almost think I . . .

> [CAPTAIN *enters, right, leaning on a stick and looking very ill.*]

CAPTAIN

Kurt, I want to talk to you. Alone!

ALICE

Is it about the safe conduct pass?

CAPTAIN

[*sitting down at the sewing-table*] Kurt, would you be kind enough to stay here with me for a while? And Alice, will you please let us have just a moment . . . of peace.

ALICE

What's the matter now? New signals! [*To* KURT.] Please sit down. [KURT *sits down reluctantly.*] And listen to the words of old age and wisdom. If a telegram arrives . . . let me know! [*Goes out, left.*]

CAPTAIN

[*with dignity, after a pause*] Have you any explanation for a fate like mine, like ours?

KURT

No, I can't explain it any more than I can explain my own!

CAPTAIN

What's the meaning of this mess-up!

KURT

In my clearer moments I've believed that that *was* the meaning, that we must submit without understanding the meaning.

CAPTAIN

To submit! Without a fixed point outside me, I can't submit!

KURT

Very well, but as a mathematician you ought to be able to find the point from the information you've been given.

CAPTAIN

I've searched for it, and—I haven't found it!

KURT

Then you've miscalculated. You must try again.

CAPTAIN

Yes, I must try again! . . . Tell me, where did you acquire all that resignation?

KURT

I've no more of it left. Don't rate me too highly.

CAPTAIN

You may have noticed that, to me, the art of living has been—elimination. In other words, wipe the slate clean and pass on. Early in life I made myself a sack; all my humiliations went into it, and when it was full I heaved it into the sea! I doubt whether any man ever suffered as many humiliations as I have. But I just wiped them off my slate and passed on, and they ceased to exist!

KURT

I've noticed how you've invented a life and an environment for yourself out of your imagination.

CAPTAIN

If I hadn't done that, how could I have gone on? How could I have put up with life? [*Puts his hand to his heart.*]

KURT

Are you feeling all right?

CAPTAIN

Not too good! [*Pause.*] There comes a time when what you call the imagination, lets you down. And then reality shows itself in all its nakedness! It's horrible! [*His voice now is an old man's, his jaw has dropped.*] You see, my friend . . . [*Controlling himself and speaking in his normal voice.*] I'm sorry! . . . When I was in town today and talked to the doctor . . . [*a sob in his voice*] . . . he said it was the end for me . . . [*in his normal voice*] . . . that I couldn't go on much longer!

KURT

Did he say that?

CAPTAIN

Yes.

KURT

It wasn't true then?

CAPTAIN

What? Oh, that—no, it wasn't true!
                    [*Pause.*]

KURT

The other things weren't true either, were they?

CAPTAIN

What other things?

KURT

About my son being posted here as a cadet!

CAPTAIN

It's the first I've heard about that.

KURT

Do you know your ability to wipe out your own misdeeds is absolutely unbelievable!

CAPTAIN

I don't know what you're talking about, old man!

KURT

Then it really *is* the end for you!

CAPTAIN

Well, there's not much left!

KURT

Listen—perhaps you never put in for that divorce that was going to disgrace your wife?

CAPTAIN

Divorce? No! Never heard of it!

KURT

[*getting up*] You admit you've been lying, then?

CAPTAIN

You use such harsh language, my friend. We should all be tolerant about each other.

KURT

So you've discovered that?

CAPTAIN

[*resolutely and in a clear voice*] Yes, I've discovered that! So forgive me, Kurt! Forgive me for everything!

KURT

That was spoken like a man! . . . But I've nothing to forgive. And I'm not the man you think I am, not any more. And I'm certainly not worthy to be your confessor.

CAPTAIN

[*in a clear voice*] Life has been so strange! So much my enemy, so vicious, that I grew vicious, too. . . . [KURT *paces up and down the room with nervous glances at the telegraph.*] What are you looking at?

KURT

Can that telegraph thing be shut off?

CAPTAIN

Well—no.

KURT

[*with growing anxiety*] Who is Sergeant-Major Östberg?

CAPTAIN

Straightforward type, eye to the main chance, of course.

KURT

And the Quartermaster?

CAPTAIN

No friend of mine, he's made that quite plain, but I've nothing to say against him.

KURT

[*looking through the window where a lantern is seen moving*] What are they doing with that lantern out there on the battery?

CAPTAIN

Is it a lantern?

KURT

Yes, and people moving about!

CAPTAIN

I should think it's what we call a fatigue party.

KURT

What's that?

CAPTAIN

A couple of men and a military policeman! Some poor fellow is being taken to the guardhouse, I should think.

KURT

Oh!

> [*Pause.*]

CAPTAIN

Now that you've got to know Alice, what do you think of her?

KURT

I can't tell. . . . I'm no good at summing people up. I understand her no more than I understand you or even myself. I'm reaching the age of wisdom, and I have to confess—I know nothing, I understand nothing. But when I see something happen, I want to know why it happened—Why did you push her into the sea?

CAPTAIN

I don't know! When I saw her on the pier it seemed to be quite natural that she should go in the water.

KURT

Have you ever felt sorry about it?

CAPTAIN

Never!

KURT

Astonishing!

CAPTAIN

Yes, it is! So astonishing that I can't believe I did it! It was a despicable thing to do.

KURT

Didn't you realize that she'd get her own back?

CAPTAIN

She's done that all right, and I find it quite natural that she should.

KURT

How did you reach your state of cynical resignation so quickly?

CAPTAIN

When I came so close to death, I saw life from a new angle. Tell me, if you were to judge between Alice and me, which of us would you say was right?

KURT

Neither of you! But I'd give you both all the compassion that's in me; you perhaps a little more than her!

CAPTAIN

Give me your hand, Kurt!

KURT

[*giving him one hand and putting the other on* THE CAPTAIN's *shoulder*] My old friend!

[ALICE *enters, left, carrying a sunshade.*]

ALICE

Well, well, well! What camaraderie! That's real friendship! Hasn't the telegram come yet?

KURT

[*coldly*] No!

ALICE

This delay makes me lose my patience, and when I lose my patience I take time by the forelock. Now watch, Kurt, I'm going to let him have the last bullet! And he'll come a cropper! . . . First I load—I learned it all from the textbook on firearms, the famous textbook "Firearms And How To Use Them" which did not even sell five thousand copies— then I take aim. [*She takes aim with the sunshade.*] Fire! How's your new wife? The young, the beautiful, the unknown one? You don't know! But I know how *my* lover is! [*She throws her arms around* KURT's *neck and kisses him. He pushes her away.*] He's all right, but he's still shy! . . . You poor wretch whom I never loved, you, who were too conceited to be jealous, you never saw how I pulled the wool over your eyes! [THE CAPTAIN *reaches forward and slashes at her with his drawn sword, but only manages to hit the furniture.*]

ALICE
>Help! Help!
>>[KURT *doesn't move.* THE CAPTAIN *collapses, still holding his sword.*]

CAPTAIN
>Judith! Avenge me!

ALICE
>Hurrah! He's dead!
>>[KURT *goes to door, back.*]

CAPTAIN
>[*struggling up*] Not yet! [*He sheathes his sword and sits down in the armchair by the sewing-table.*] Judith! Judith!

ALICE
>[*going towards* KURT] I'm leaving here—with you!

KURT
>[*pushing her away so that she falls to her knees*] Go to the hell you came from! Goodbye forever! [*Goes to door.*]

CAPTAIN
>Don't leave me, Kurt. She'll kill me!

ALICE
>Kurt! Don't desert me, don't desert us!

KURT
>Goodbye! [*Goes.*]

ALICE
>[*volte-face*] The villain! There's a friend for you!

CAPTAIN
>[*gently*] Forgive me, Alice, and come here! Come quickly!

ALICE
>[*going to* THE CAPTAIN] That must be the biggest villain and worst hypocrite I ever met in all my life! At least, you're a man! I give you that!

CAPTAIN
>Alice, listen! . . . I can't live much longer!

ALICE
>Is that true?

CAPTAIN
>The doctor told me.

ALICE
>Then all the other things you said were untrue as well?

CAPTAIN
>Yes.

ALICE

[*beside herself*] Oh! What have I done? . . .

CAPTAIN

Everything can be put right!

ALICE

No! It's gone too far!

CAPTAIN

There's nothing that can't be put right if only you wipe the slate clean and pass on.

ALICE

But the telegram! The telegram!

CAPTAIN

What telegram?

ALICE

[*on her knees by* THE CAPTAIN] Is it the end for us? Must it happen? I've caught myself in my own trap, caught both of us. Why did you have to tell all those lies? And why did that man have to come here and tempt me! . . . We are lost! Everything could have been put right, everything could have been forgiven if only you had had the generosity of spirit!

CAPTAIN

What is it that can't be forgiven? What haven't I forgiven you for?

ALICE

It's true, but this has gone too far.

CAPTAIN

I can't guess what you're driving at, though I know how cleverly you can think up your infernal plots. . . .

ALICE

Oh, if I could get out of this! If only I could get out of this, I'd look after you. . . . Edgar, I'd love you!

CAPTAIN

Just listen! . . . What's happening to me?

ALICE

There's not a soul who could help us . . . no, no one alive can do it!

CAPTAIN

Well then, who?

ALICE

[*looking* THE CAPTAIN *in the eyes*] I don't know! What will become of the children with their name dishonoured?

CAPTAIN

Their name dishonoured? What have you done?

ALICE

Not I! Not I! . . . Judith will have to leave school! And when she goes out into the world, she'll be as lonely as we are. And as vindictive! . . . So you didn't see Judith, either, did you?

CAPTAIN

No! But you can wipe that off the slate, too.

[*The telegraph taps.* ALICE *jumps up.*]

ALICE

[*crying*] Now for the disaster! [*To* THE CAPTAIN.] Don't listen to it!

CAPTAIN

[*calmly*] I don't intend to listen to it, my dear, so calm yourself! . . .

ALICE

[*by the telegraph, standing on her toes to see out of the window*] Don't listen! Don't listen!

CAPTAIN

[*his hands over his ears*] I'm holding my ears, Lisa, my child!

ALICE

[*on her knees with raised arms*] God, help us! . . . The fatigue party is coming. . . . [*Crying vehemently.*] God in Heaven! [*Her lips move in silent prayer. The telegraph goes on tapping and a long strip of paper emerges. Silence.* ALICE *gets up, tears off the paper strip and reads it to herself. Then she raises her eyes, goes to* THE CAPTAIN *and kisses him on the forehead.*] It's all over—it was nothing! [*She sits down in the other chair and sobs into her handkerchief.*]

CAPTAIN

What is the secret you've got there?

ALICE

Don't ask me! It's over now!

CAPTAIN

Just as you like, dear!

ALICE

You wouldn't have spoken to me like that three days ago. Why have you changed?

CAPTAIN

Well, my dear, when I collapsed the first time, I was on the other side of the grave. What I saw, I have forgotten, but the impression is still with me.

ALICE

Impression?

CAPTAIN

The hope—of better things!

ALICE

Better things?

CAPTAIN

Yes, that this is life itself, I've never really believed. . . . This is death! Or something even worse. . . .

ALICE

And we . . . ?

CAPTAIN

. . . must have been set the task of torturing each other . . . at least, that's what it looks like!

ALICE

Haven't we tortured each other enough?

CAPTAIN

Yes, I think so! And look at the chaos! [*Looking round him.*] How about putting things right now? And cleaning the place up?

ALICE

[*getting up*] Yes, if it's possible!

CAPTAIN

[*looking round in the room*] It can't be done in a single day! And it won't!

ALICE

In two, then! Many days!

CAPTAIN

Let's hope so. [*Pause. Sitting down again.*] So you didn't free yourself this time! But you didn't get me locked up, either! [ALICE *looks surprised.*] Yes, I knew you were plotting to put me in prison, but I'm wiping it off your slate. . . . You've done worse things than that, haven't you? . . . [ALICE *is speechless.*] I never swindled my men—I was innocent.

ALICE

And now it's your idea that I should become your nurse?

CAPTAIN

If you want to!

ALICE

What else can I do?

CAPTAIN

I don't know.

ALICE

[*sitting down in despair*] Why, these must be the eternal torments! Is there no end then?

CAPTAIN

Yes, if we are patient! Perhaps when death comes, life begins.

ALICE

Oh, if that were true!

CAPTAIN

Do you think Kurt was a hypocrite?

ALICE

Yes, I'm sure he was!

CAPTAIN

I don't think so! But everyone who gets close to us becomes evil and goes his way. . . . Kurt was weak, and evil is strong! [*Pause.*]
Life is dull nowadays! In the past, you hit out; now you only shake your fist! I'd almost bet my boots that in three months' time we'll be celebrating our silver wedding . . . with Kurt as best man. . . . The Doctor and Gerda will be there. . . . The Quartermaster will make the speech and the Sergeant-Major will be the cheerleader! And if I know the Colonel, he'll invite himself! Yes, you can laugh! But do you remember Adolf's silver wedding . . . the fellow in the Rifles? The bride had to wear the ring on her right hand because the bridegroom, in one of his tender moments, had chopped off her left ring finger with a billhook.
[ALICE *holds the handkerchief to her face to hide her laughter.*]
Are you crying? No, you must be laughing! . . . Yes, my child, sometimes we cry, sometimes we laugh! Which is the best thing to do . . . don't ask me! . . . The other day I read in a newspaper that a man who had been divorced seven times—that is to say he'd had seven wives—finally went off with wife number one and married her again. He was ninety-eight! That's love. . . . Whether life is serious or just a joke, I can't make it out! It can be most agonizing when it's a joke, and most enjoyable and serene when it's serious. . . . But when, eventually, you try to take it seriously, then somebody comes along and takes a rise out of you. Example, Kurt! . . . Do you want a silver wedding? [ALICE *doesn't reply.*] Say yes, won't you! They'll laugh at us, but what does it matter! We'll laugh too, or we'll be serious, as the case may be!

ALICE

Yes, we'll have it.

CAPTAIN

[*seriously*] So be it! A silver wedding! . . . [*Getting up.*] Wipe our slates clean and pass on! We're going to pass on!

THE DANCE OF DEATH

PART II

CHARACTERS

EDGAR

ALICE

KURT

ALLAN, *Kurt's son*

JUDITH, *daughter of Edgar and Alice*

THE LIEUTENANT

An oval drawing room in white and gold. In the back wall, open French windows through which the terrace of the garden can be seen. The terrace is a public promenade with stone balustrade along which are blue and white faïence-pots with petunias and scarlet geraniums. In the background is the shore battery with sentry on guard; in the distance, the open sea.

In the drawing room, left, a gilded sofa with table and chairs. Right, a grand piano, a desk and a fireplace. In the foreground, an American easy chair. Beside the desk, a copper standard lamp attached to a table. On the walls, various old oil paintings.

Scene One

A warm summer morning. ALLAN *is at the desk, studying.*

    JUDITH *enters through the open French windows. She is wearing a short summer dress, her hair is in a plait; her hat is in one hand, her tennis racket in the other. She stops at the door.* ALLAN *stands up courteously.*

JUDITH

[*seriously but friendly*] Why don't you come out and have a game of tennis?

ALLAN

[*shyly, trying to hide his emotion*] I've got work to do. . . .

JUDITH

Didn't you see that I'd left my bike facing the oak tree and not backing away from it?

ALLAN

Yes, I did!

JUDITH

Well, what does that mean?

ALLAN

It means . . . that you want me to play tennis . . . but there's my work. . . . I've got some problems to solve . . . and your father's quite a severe taskmaster. . . .

JUDITH

Do you like him?

ALLAN

Yes, I do! He takes an interest in all his pupils.

JUDITH

He takes an interest in everybody and everything. . . . Are you coming?

ALLAN

You know I'd like to, but I can't.

JUDITH

I'll ask my father to let you off homework.

ALLAN

Don't do that! It'll start people talking!

JUDITH

I can handle him all right. What I want—he wants.

ALLAN

That's probably because you're so hard!

JUDITH

You ought to be hard too!

ALLAN

I'm not one of the wolf family!

JUDITH

Then you're a sheep!

ALLAN

I'd prefer that!

JUDITH

Tell me, why won't you come and play tennis?

ALLAN

You know why. . . .

JUDITH

All the same, I'd like you to tell me. . . . The Lieutenant . . .

ALLAN

You don't care a damn about me, but you don't care for the Lieutenant's company either—unless I'm there, too—so that you can watch me suffering.

JUDITH

Am I as cruel as that? I didn't know!

ALLAN

Well, you know now!

JUDITH

Then I'll mend my ways. I don't want to be cruel, I don't want to be bad. Not in your eyes.

ALLAN

You're only saying that so that you can lord it over me. I'm your slave already, but that's not enough for you. The slave must be tortured and thrown to the wild beasts! You've got the other fellow in your clutches so why do you bother with me? Let me go my way, and you go yours!

JUDITH

Are you showing me the door? [ALLAN *doesn't answer.*] All right, I'll go! We're cousins so we'll have to meet now and then, but I won't go out of my way! [ALLAN *sits down at the desk again and returns to his work. Instead of going,* JUDITH *gradually edges towards him.*] Don't be nervous. I'll be off in a minute. . . . I just wanted to see how well off the Quarantine Officer is. . . . [*Looking round.*] White and gold!— A Bechstein grand. Well, well—We're still in the tower even though my father's retired—the tower where my mother's had to live for twenty-five years . . . and we're there on charity at that! You're rich, you . . .

ALLAN

[*calmly*] We're not!

JUDITH

So you say, but you're always well dressed—although you look good no matter what you wear! . . . Did you hear what I said? [*Draws closer.*]

ALLAN

I heard.

JUDITH

How can you hear and do your sums at the same time—or whatever it is you're doing?

ALLAN

I don't hear with my eyes!

JUDITH

Your eyes! Oh! . . . Have you ever looked at them in a mirror?

ALLAN

Go away.

JUDITH

You despise me, don't you?

ALLAN

My dear girl, I don't even bother to think about you!

JUDITH

[*edging still nearer*] Archimedes doing his sums, when along comes the soldier and runs him through the body! [*Ruffles his papers with her racket.*]

ALLAN

Leave my papers alone.

JUDITH

Archimedes said that, too! And now I've a fancy that you're imagining things! You're thinking I can't live without you.

ALLAN

Why can't you leave me alone?

JUDITH

If you'd only behave politely, I'd help you with your exams.

ALLAN

You?

JUDITH

Yes, I know the examiners. . . .

ALLAN

[*sternly*] And supposing you do?

JUDITH

Don't you understand that you should be in your teachers' good books?

ALLAN

You mean your father and the Lieutenant?

JUDITH

And the Colonel!

ALLAN

Are you telling me that under your protection I could dodge my work?

JUDITH

You're a bad translator. . . .

ALLAN

Of a bad original. . . .

JUDITH

You ought to be ashamed of yourself!

ALLAN

I am—and of you! . . . I'm ashamed of having listened to you! Why don't you go?

JUDITH

Because I know how much you enjoy being with me. Somehow or other you're always passing by my window. Something always takes you to town on the same boat as me. You can't go out sailing unless I'm there to be your crew.

ALLAN

[*shyly*] A youngster like you shouldn't talk like that!

JUDITH

Do you think I'm still a child?

ALLAN

Sometimes you're an angelic child, sometimes a wicked woman! You seem to have picked me out to be your sheep.

JUDITH

You *are* a sheep; that's why I'm going to protect you!

ALLAN

[*getting up*] The wolf makes a bad shepherd, doesn't he? You want to eat me . . . that's it, isn't it? You want to barter your lovely eyes for my head.

JUDITH

Oh, so you *have* noticed my eyes? I didn't think you had it in you!
          [ALLAN *collects his papers and starts to go out, right.* JUDITH
          bars his way in front of the door.]

ALLAN

Get out of my way, or . . .

JUDITH

Or?

ALLAN

If you were a man, I'd . . . But you're just a slip of a girl!

JUDITH

And so?

ALLAN

If you had any pride in you, you'd have made yourself scarce. . . . It's obvious you're not wanted here!

JUDITH

I'll get my own back for that!

ALLAN

I can well believe it!

JUDITH

[*going towards exit, back, furious*] I'll—get—my—own—back—for—that!
[*Goes out.*]

KURT

[*entering, left*] Where are you off to, Allan?

ALLAN

Oh, is that you?

KURT

Who was that who went out like a whirlwind? The bushes trembled!

ALLAN

It was Judith!

KURT

She *is* a bit hot-headed, but she's a nice girl!

ALLAN

When a girl is cruel and bad-tempered, she's always said to be a nice girl!

KURT

You mustn't be so hard, Allan. Don't you like your new relatives?

ALLAN

> I like Uncle Edgar. . . .

KURT

> Yes, he has lots of good points. . . . What about your other teachers? The Lieutenant, for instance?

ALLAN

> He's so temperamental! Sometimes, I think he's got it in for me.

KURT

> Nonsense! . . . You go around getting ideas about people. Stop brooding, do the right thing, mind your own business, and let other people mind theirs!

ALLAN

> That's what I do, but . . . they won't leave you alone! They draw you in . . . just like the cuttlefish down by the pier . . . they don't bite you, but they stir up whirlpools that suck you in. . . .

KURT

> [*kindly*] I think you're too inclined to look on the dark side of things. Don't you like it here with me? Is there anything you miss?

ALLAN

> I've never had such a good time, but . . . there's something here that's suffocating me!

KURT

> What, here by the sea? Don't you like the sea?

ALLAN

> Yes, the open sea! But on the beaches, there's seaweed, cuttlefish, jellyfish, nettlefish or whatever they're called. . . .

KURT

> You're indoors too much! Go out and play tennis!

ALLAN

> That's not much fun!

KURT

> You're annoyed with Judith, aren't you!

ALLAN

> Judith?

KURT

> You're so fastidious about people; you mustn't be. It only makes you lonely!

ALLAN

> I'm not fastidious, but . . . I feel as if I were at the bottom of a pile of logs, waiting for my turn to go into the fire. . . . I'm weighed down, weighed down by everything that's on top of me. . . .

KURT

Wait till it's your turn. The pile's getting less and less. . . .

ALLAN

Yes, but so slowly, so slowly! . . . And in the meantime, I'm getting mouldy!

KURT

It's no fun to be young! And yet people envy you your youth!

ALLAN

Do they? Would you change places?

KURT

No thanks!

ALLAN

Do you know what the worst thing is? It's to sit still and keep your mouth shut while your elders are talking piffle. I may know a damn sight more than they do on some topic—and yet I have to keep a still tongue in my head. Oh, I'm sorry, I wasn't referring to you as one of my elders.

KURT

But why not?

ALLAN

Perhaps because we've only just got to know each other.

KURT

And because . . . your ideas about me aren't what they used to be?

ALLAN

That's right.

KURT

During the years when we were separated, I suppose you didn't always feel very friendly towards me?

ALLAN

No!

KURT

Did you ever see any pictures of me?

ALLAN

One, and it wasn't flattering!

KURT

It made me look old?

ALLAN

Yes!

KURT

Ten years ago, my hair went grey overnight. Now it's gone dark again without any help from me. Let's talk about other things. Look, here comes my cousin. She's Aunt Alice to you. What do you think of her?

ALLAN

I'd rather not say.

KURT

Then I won't ask!

> [ALICE *enters wearing a very light summer frock. She is carrying a sunshade.*]

ALICE

Good morning, Kurt! [*Gives him a look indicating that* ALLAN *should leave.*]

KURT

[*to* ALLAN] Leave us, will you!

> [ALLAN *goes out, right.* ALICE *sits on sofa, left.* KURT *takes a chair near her.*]

ALICE

[*confused*] He'll be here soon, so you needn't feel embarrassed!

KURT

Why should I?

ALICE

With your prim ideas. . . .

KURT

They only apply to me.

ALICE

Well! . . . I forgot myself once, when I saw my liberator in you, but you kept your head . . . so we may as well forget—what never happened.

KURT

Let's forget it then!

ALICE

I don't think *he* has forgotten. . . .

KURT

You mean the night he had that heart attack . . . and you whooped with delight too soon because you thought he was dead?

ALICE

Yes, but he's quite recovered now. When he gave up drinking he learned to hold his tongue, and now he's more terrible than ever. Not long before our silver wedding, he seemed to have turned over a new leaf. He was calling me "my dear" and "my child" and even "my darling." He was my lover again, the man I knew in his youth. Fool that I was to be taken in! That silver wedding was a ruse to impress the island. As soon as it was over, he reverted. He's up to something, but I don't know what. . . .

KURT

Alice, your husband is a good-natured booby, who has done me lots of good turns. . . .

ALICE

Beware of his good turns. I know them!

KURT

Oh, come now!

ALICE

So he's taken you in, too! Can't you see the danger, can't you see the traps he lays?

KURT

No!

ALICE

Then you're doomed!

KURT

Oh, for heaven's sake!

ALICE

I sit here, watching disaster steal up on you like a cat. . . . I point it out, but you can't see it!

KURT

Allan can't see it, either, and his views are not prejudiced. As a matter of fact, all he can see is Judith, but that's always a guarantee of good relations, isn't it?

ALICE

Do you know Judith?

KURT

A little flirt, with a plait down her back and skirts that are a bit too short! . . .

ALICE

That's right! But the other day I saw her in a long skirt. . . . She was a young lady then . . . well, not so young, with her hair up!

KURT

I admit she's a bit precocious!

ALICE

And she's just playing with Allan!

KURT

That's all right, as long as it's only play.

ALICE

So you think it's all right! . . . Edgar will be here soon, he'll sit in the easy chair—he's taken such a fancy to it he could walk off with it.

KURT

He can have it!

ALICE

Let him sit there; we'll stay here. And while he's talking—in the mornings, he goes on and on—while he's chattering about trivialities, I'll decipher them for you! . . .

KURT

Oh dear! You see too much, my dear Alice, much too much! What have I got to be afraid of as long as I run my Quarantine Station effectively and behave decently otherwise?

ALICE

You believe in justice and honour and all that?

KURT

Yes, experience has taught me to. There was a time when I believed the very opposite. It cost me dear!

ALICE

Here he is! . . .

KURT

I've never seen you so nervous before!

ALICE

My courage was only ignorance of the danger!

KURT

The danger? . . . You'll be making me nervous soon.

ALICE

I wish I could. . . . There!

> [THE CAPTAIN *enters, back, in a black frock coat, buttoned-up, and army cap. He carries a silver-topped cane. He greets them with a nod, crosses to the easy chair and sits in it.*]

ALICE

[*to* KURT] Let him speak first!

CAPTAIN

This is a beautiful chair you've got here, my dear Kurt! Quite beautiful!

KURT

It's yours, if you'll accept it as a gift.

CAPTAIN

I didn't mean that. . . .

KURT

But I did. Just think what you've done for me!

CAPTAIN

[*exuberantly*] Oh, nonsense! . . . When I'm sitting here, I can see the whole island, all the promenades, all the people on their verandahs, all the ships docking or going out to sea. . . . You really have discovered the best part of the island, and it's hardly one of the Isles of the Blessed. Is it, Alice? . . . They call it "Little Hell," but Kurt has built himself a paradise here. No Eve, of course, because when she turned up, that was the end of Paradise! I say, did you know that this used to be a royal hunting lodge?

KURT

So I've heard!

CAPTAIN

You live royally enough here, but—dare I say it—you owe it all to me!

ALICE

[*to* KURT] There you are, he'll get what he can out of you!

KURT

I owe you a great deal.

CAPTAIN

Oh, fiddlesticks! Tell me, did those cases of wine arrive?

KURT

Yes!

CAPTAIN

And you're pleased with them?

KURT

Delighted. I'd like you to congratulate your wine merchant on my behalf.

CAPTAIN

His wines are always best vintage.

ALICE

[*to* KURT] And his prices second-best—you pay the difference. . . .

CAPTAIN

What did you say, Alice?

ALICE

I? Nothing!

CAPTAIN

Yes! When this Quarantine Station was first mooted, I thought of putting in for the job. . . . I even made a study of quarantine systems.

ALICE

[*to* KURT] He's lying!

CAPTAIN

[*bragging*] I didn't share the Council's old-fashioned ideas about disinfectants. You see, I was all on the side of the Neptunists—we called them that, because they preferred the water method. . . .

KURT

I beg your pardon, but I was the one who propagated the water method. At the time you were all for combustion.

CAPTAIN

Me? What nonsense!

ALICE

[*aloud*] I remember that, too!

CAPTAIN

You?

KURT

I remember it all the better . . .

CAPTAIN

[*interrupting*] That may be so, but it's immaterial. . . . [*Raising his voice.*] However . . . we have now reached the stage where a new state of affairs . . . [*to* KURT, *who is trying to interrupt*] . . . if you please . . . has arisen. . . . Tremendous advances in the whole quarantine system are about to take place. . . .

KURT

By the way, do you know who's writing those idiotic articles in the paper?

CAPTAIN

[*flushing*] I don't know, but why do you call them idiotic?

ALICE

[*to* KURT] Careful! He wrote them!

KURT

[*to* ALICE] He? . . . [*To* THE CAPTAIN.] Well then—not well-informed.

CAPTAIN

Who are you to judge, anyway?

ALICE

Are you going to start quarreling now?

KURT

I'm not.

CAPTAIN

It's hard enough to get on with anyone on this island, but it's up to us to set an example. . . .

KURT

I agree, but can you explain this to me? When I came here, I was soon on good terms with all the officials. I was particularly close to the attorney, as close as men of our age can get. Then, after a while—it was soon after you got better—one after another, they started to snub me, and yesterday the attorney cut me dead on the promenade. I can't tell you how it upset me. [CAPTAIN *doesn't answer.*] Have they turned against you, too?

CAPTAIN

No, just the reverse.

ALICE

[*to* KURT] Don't you understand—he's stolen your friends from you!

KURT

[*to* THE CAPTAIN] I wondered if it was because I wouldn't subscribe to that issue of new shares.

CAPTAIN

No, no! But can you tell me why you wouldn't subscribe?

KURT

Because I'd already invested the little bit I had in your soda factory! And also because a new issue means that the old shares can't be very healthy.

CAPTAIN

[*absent-mindedly*] That's a beautiful lamp you've got there! Where did you pick it up?

KURT

In town, of course.

ALICE

[*to* KURT] Don't let that lamp out of your sight, Kurt.

KURT

[*to* THE CAPTAIN] You mustn't think I'm ungrateful or that I don't trust your judgment, Edgar.

CAPTAIN

It doesn't show much trust when you want to get out of a concern you helped to found.

KURT

My dear man, ordinary common sense advises anyone to save what he has while he can!

CAPTAIN

Save? Where's the danger? Who's going to rob you?

KURT

Why get so heated about it?

CAPTAIN

Weren't you satisfied when I helped you invest your money at six per cent?

KURT

Yes, I was most grateful!

CAPTAIN

You're *not* grateful—it's not in your nature, but you can't help *that*!

ALICE

[*to* KURT] *Listen* to *him*!

KURT

I'm anything but perfect and my efforts to improve haven't been too successful, but I do acknowledge obligations. . . .

CAPTAIN

Show it then! [*Stretches out his hand and picks up newspaper.*] I say, look at this! Look what it says! . . . An obituary! [*Reads.*] The Medical Officer of Health is dead!

ALICE

[*to* KURT] He's speculating on the corpse already.

CAPTAIN

[*as if to himself*] This will mean . . . certain . . . changes.

KURT

In what way?

CAPTAIN

[*getting up*] That's what we've got to find out, isn't it?

ALICE

[*to* THE CAPTAIN] Where are you going?

CAPTAIN

I ought to go into town! [*Catches sight of a letter on the desk, picks it up as if absent-mindedly, reads the address, and puts it back.*] I'm sorry. I'm so absent-minded.

KURT

No harm done!

CAPTAIN

There are Allan's instruments! Where *is* the boy?

KURT

Out. With the girls.

CAPTAIN

The big lout! I'm not happy about it. And Judith shouldn't be running around like that. . . . You must keep an eye on your young gentleman, and I'll take care of my young lady! [*He picks out a few notes on the grand piano as he passes it.*] Lovely tone! A Steinbech, eh?

KURT

Bechstein!

CAPTAIN

Yes, you're comfortably off, aren't you? Thanks to me—who got you the job!

ALICE

[*to* KURT] That's a lie! He tried to stop you from coming here!

CAPTAIN

Goodbye for the present! I'm taking the next steamer. [*He has a good look at the pictures on the walls as he goes out.*]

ALICE

Well?

KURT

Well?

ALICE

He's plotting something but I don't know what it is yet. Tell me— that envelope he looked at . . . who was it from?

KURT

I'm afraid it was a secret—my only one.

ALICE

And he guessed it! I told you—he's a magician. . . . Is anything printed on the envelope?

KURT

Yes, it says "The Radical Party Headquarters."

ALICE

So he's discovered your secret. You're thinking of standing for Parliament, aren't you? Well, it wouldn't surprise me if he takes your place.

KURT

Has he ever thought about it in the past?

ALICE

No, but he's thinking about it now. I read it in his face while he was looking at the envelope.

KURT

Is that why he's going to town?

ALICE

No, he made up his mind about that when he saw the obituary announcement!

KURT

What can he hope to gain from the death of the Medical Officer of Health?

ALICE

Who can tell? The man might have been an enemy of his. He might have been interfering with his plans.

KURT

If he's as terrible as you say, there's good reason for fearing him!

ALICE

You heard him, didn't you—how he wanted to get you in his power, to tie you hand and foot, because of obligations that don't exist. For example, he never got you the job here; on the contrary, he tried to stop it. He's a man-eater, an insect, a sort of woodworm that will devour your inside till one day you're as hollow as a rotten fir tree. . . . He hates you, but he's bound to you because he remembers your past friendship.

KURT

What insight we get when we hate!

ALICE

And how silly we are when we're in love! Blind and silly!

KURT

Whew, what are you saying!

ALICE

You know what a vampire is, don't you? It's the soul of a dead person trying to find a home in a living body. It's a parasite. Edgar is dead. He's been dead ever since he had that fall that time! You know he has no interests of his own, no real personality, no real initiative. But let him get hold of some other man and he'll cling tight, dig down with his suckers and start to grow and bear fruit. You're the man he's going to cling to now.

KURT

If he gets too close, I'll shake him off!

ALICE

Shake off a limpet! You'll see! . . . Listen, do you know why he doesn't want Judith and Allan to be together?

KURT

I suppose he's nervous that their feelings might get the better of them.

ALICE

Not at all! . . . He wants to marry Judith to . . . the Colonel!

KURT

[*upset*] That old widower?

ALICE

Yes.

KURT

It's disgusting! . . . And Judith?

ALICE

If she could get the General, who's eighty, she'd jump at him in order to humiliate the Colonel, who's sixty. To humiliate, you see, that's her aim in life! To trample and humiliate, that's the motto of *that* family!

KURT

Is Judith really like that? That lovely, proud, splendid creature!

ALICE

Yes, we know all about that! Do you mind if I write a letter here?

KURT

[*tidying his desk*] Here you are!

ALICE

[*taking off her gloves and sitting down at the desk*] Now I'm going to try my hand at the art of war! I failed once, when I tried to kill my dragon! But I've learned a lot since then!

KURT

You know you have to load before you shoot, don't you?

ALICE

Yes, and with ball cartridges, what's more.

> [KURT *exits right.* ALICE *thinks for a while, then starts to write.* ALLAN *dashes in. He does not notice* ALICE. *He throws himself down on the sofa and buries his face in his arms. A lace handkerchief is crunched in his hand.* ALICE *watches him for a while, then she gets up and goes to the sofa.*]

ALICE

[*gently*] Allan!

> [*He sits up, embarrassed, hiding the handkerchief behind his back.*]

ALICE

[*gently, womanly, with deep feeling*] You mustn't be afraid of me, Allan, you're in no danger from me. . . . What's the matter? . . . Are you ill?

ALLAN

Yes!

ALICE

What is it?

ALLAN

I don't know!

ALICE

Have you got a headache?

ALLAN

No-o!

ALICE

Is it your heart? Pain?

ALLAN

Ye-es!

ALICE

Agony, agony, as though your heart were melting away! And it pulls, pulls . . .

ALLAN

How do you know?

ALICE

And you want to die, you wish you were dead, everything is so impossible. And you can only think of one thing . . . one person . . . but if two people can only think of this one person, then sorrow is unbearable for one of them. . . . [ALLAN *begins to pluck absent-mindedly at the handkerchief.*]
That's the sickness that nobody can cure . . . you can't eat, you can't drink, you only want to weep, and how bitterly you weep . . . you hide away in the woods so that nobody can see you, because this is the grief other people laugh at—people are so cruel! Whew! What do you want of her? Nothing! You don't want to kiss her lips, because you think you'd die if you did! Whenever your thoughts fly to her you feel death bearing down on you. And it is death, my child, the death that gives life. But you don't understand that yet! There's a smell of violets. It's she! [*She goes up to* ALLAN *and gently takes the handkerchief.*] It's she, she's everywhere, only she! Oh, oh, oh! [ALLAN *can do nothing but hide his face in* ALICE'S *arms.*]
Poor boy, poor boy! Oh, how it hurts, how it hurts! [*She dabs his face with the handkerchief.*] There, now! Cry, have your cry, that's right! You'll feel easier! . . . And now, get up, Allan and be a man, or she won't look at you! That cruel girl who isn't cruel! Has she been tormenting you?—With the Lieutenant? Listen, my boy! You must make friends with the Lieutenant, then you can discuss her with one another! That'll give you a bit of comfort, too!

ALLAN

I don't want to have anything to do with the Lieutenant!

ALICE

Listen, little boy! It won't be long before the Lieutenant calls on you to talk about her! Because . . . [ALLAN *looks up with a gleam of hope.*] Well, shall I be nice and tell you something? [ALLAN *bows his head.*] He's as unhappy as you are!

ALLAN

[*radiant*] No?

ALICE

Yes, and he needs someone so that he can bare his soul when Judith has been unkind to him. You've recovered very quickly.

ALLAN

Doesn't she want the Lieutenant?

ALICE

She doesn't want you either, my love. It's the Colonel she's after!
[ALLAN's *face falls.*] What? It's raining again. No, you don't get this
handkerchief back because Judith takes great care of her belongings
and wants her dozen complete! [ALLAN *looks disheartened.*] Yes, that's
the way Judith is! . . . Now sit there while I write another letter, then
you can run an errand for me! [*She goes to the desk and writes.*]

> [THE LIEUTENANT *enters, back. He looks melancholy but it
> is not the melancholy that can be ridiculous. He does not
> notice* ALICE *but goes straight across to* ALLAN.]

LIEUTENANT

Cadet! [ALLAN *gets up and stands at attention.*] Don't get up!

> [ALICE *watches them.* THE LIEUTENANT *sits by* ALLAN's *side.
> He sighs, takes out a handkerchief similar to the other one
> and wipes his brow.* ALLAN *looks at the handkerchief greed-
> ily.* THE LIEUTENANT *looks at* ALLAN *sadly.* ALICE *coughs.*
> THE LIEUTENANT *springs to attention.*]

ALICE

Sit down, do!

LIEUTENANT

I beg your pardon, ma'am.

ALICE

That's quite all right! . . . Please sit down and make the Cadet feel
more at home. He's a bit lost here on the island. [*She writes.*]

LIEUTENANT

[*somewhat put out, talking to* ALLAN *in an undertone*] It's awfully hot,
don't you think?

ALLAN

Oh yes, awfully!

LIEUTENANT

Have you finished the sixth book yet?

ALLAN

I'm on the last proposition now.

LIEUTENANT

It's a nasty one, isn't it! [*Silence.*] Have you . . . [*searching for words*]
. . . had any tennis today?

ALLAN

No, it was too hot in the sun!

LIEUTENANT

[*in despair, but without becoming comical*] Yes, it's awfully hot today!

ALLAN

[*whispering*] Awfully hot!
                    [*Silence.*]

LIEUTENANT

Have you . . . been out sailing today?

ALLAN

No, I couldn't find anybody to go with me.

LIEUTENANT

Would you . . . trust *me?*

ALLAN

[*respectfully, as before*] That would be too great an honour for me, sir.

LIEUTENANT

Oh, not at all. . . . Do you think . . . the wind will be all right today, this afternoon, say, because that's the only time I'm free.

ALLAN

[*slyly*] The wind drops in the afternoon, and . . . that's when Miss Judith has her lessons. . . .

LIEUTENANT

Oh! Is that so? Hm!—Do you think . . .

ALICE

Would either of you young gentlemen deliver a letter for me . . . [ALLAN *and* THE LIEUTENANT *look at each other distrustfully*] . . . to Miss Judith?
[ALLAN *and* THE LIEUTENANT *jump up together and rush towards* ALICE, *but they retain a certain dignity in their efforts to hide their feelings.*] Both of you? That'll ensure its arrival! [*She gives the letter to* THE LIEUTENANT.]
Lieutenant, will you let me have that handkerchief? My daughter takes great care of her belongings! She's rather mean. . . . Give me the handkerchief! . . . I don't want to laugh at you, but you mustn't make fools of yourselves unnecessarily. And the Colonel doesn't see himself as Othello! [*She takes the handkerchief.*]
Off you go now, both of you, and try to hide your feelings, as well as you can! [THE LIEUTENANT *bows and goes, with* ALLAN *close on his heels.*]

ALICE

[*calling out*] Allan!

ALLAN

[*stopping very reluctantly in the door*] Yes, Aunt Alice?

ALICE

Stay here! Unless you want to do yourself more harm than you can bear.

ALLAN

Yes, but he's on his way!

ALICE

Let him stew in his own juice! But you take care!

ALLAN

I don't want to take care!

ALICE

Then you'll have a good cry later and I'll have to go to the trouble of mothering you all over again.

ALLAN

I want to go!

ALICE

All right then, go! But come back here, my young Don Quixote, and I'll have the right to laugh at you!

> [ALLAN *runs out after* THE LIEUTENANT. ALICE *starts writing again. Enter* KURT.]

KURT

Alice, I've had an anonymous letter. It's very worrying.

ALICE

Have you noticed that Edgar has become a different man since he gave up wearing his uniform? I never thought a coat had so much influence!

KURT

You didn't answer my question!

ALICE

It wasn't a question! It was a piece of information! What's worrying you?

KURT

Everything!

ALICE

He went to town! His trips to town always bring something terrible in their wake.

KURT

There's nothing I can do because I don't know where the attack's coming from.

ALICE

[*folding up the letter*] We'll see if I've guessed it or not! . . .

KURT

Will you help me then?

ALICE

Yes! . . . But only as far as it concerns me . . . that's to say, my children!

KURT

That's understood! . . . Listen, how silent it is, nature, the sea, everywhere!

ALICE

But beyond the silence, I can hear voices, murmuring, cries!

KURT

Ssh! I can hear something, too. . . . No, it was only the seagulls!

ALICE

But *I* can hear other things! . . . And now I'm off to the post office—with this letter!

Scene Two

Scene: The same. ALLAN *is at the desk, working.* JUDITH *is in the door-way, wearing a hat for tennis and holding the handle-bars of a bicycle.*

JUDITH
May I borrow your bicycle wrench?

ALLAN
[*without looking up*] No, you may not!

JUDITH
You're only being rude because I'm being nice to you.

ALLAN
[*not snappishly*] I'm not being anything at all; all I ask is to be left alone!

JUDITH
[*drawing nearer*] Allan!

ALLAN
Well?

JUDITH
You mustn't be angry with me!

ALLAN
I'm not!

JUDITH
Your hand on it!

ALLAN
I'm not going to shake hands, but I'm not angry. What do you want with me, anyway?

JUDITH

Oh, you're so silly!

ALLAN

That's quite likely!

JUDITH

You think I'm quite awful.

ALLAN

No, I know you're quite nice. You can be, anyhow.

JUDITH

Well, you can't blame me if you and the Lieutenant go creeping around
in the woods, crying your eyes out. What have you got to cry for, anyway? [ALLAN *is embarrassed.*] Look at me! . . . I never cry. And why
are you such good chums now? What do you talk about when you walk
around arm in arm?

[ALLAN *is at a loss for an answer.*]

JUDITH

Allan! You'll soon see the sort of person I am, and what I can do for
people I'm fond of! And let me give you a piece of advice . . . though
I don't like to tell tales out of doors. . . . Be on your guard!

ALLAN

What for?

JUDITH

Trouble!

ALLAN

Where's it coming from?

JUDITH

Where you'd least expect it!

ALLAN

I'm quite used to trouble. Life hasn't been a bed of roses for me . . .
what's in the wind now?

JUDITH

[*thoughtfully*] You poor boy! . . . Give me your hand! [ALLAN *gives
her his hand.*] Look at me! . . . Are you afraid to look at me?

[ALLAN *hurries out, left, in order to hide his feelings.* THE
LIEUTENANT *enters, back.*]

LIEUTENANT

I'm sorry! I thought the Cadet . . .

JUDITH

Listen, Lieutenant, would you like to be my friend? My confidant?

LIEUTENANT

If you'd honour me like that. . . .

JUDITH

It's only this. . . . Don't let Allan down when the bad news comes!

LIEUTENANT

What bad news?

JUDITH

You'll know soon; today, perhaps! . . . Do you like Allan?

LIEUTENANT

He's my best pupil but I value him personally because of his strength of character. . . . Yes, there are moments in life when you need [*with emphasis*] strength—strength to bear up, to go on—in a word, to suffer!

JUDITH

That was more than a word, wasn't it! . . . However, you do like Allan, don't you?

LIEUTENANT

Yes!

JUDITH

Go and find him and keep him company. . . .

LIEUTENANT

That's why I'm here, for *that* and *nothing* else! I had no other object in calling!

JUDITH

I hadn't supposed you had—not of the kind you mean! . . . Allan went that way. [*She points, left.*]

LIEUTENANT

[*going left, unwillingly*] Yes. . . . I'll do that!

JUDITH

Do, please!

        [ALICE *enters, back.*]

ALICE

What are you doing here?

JUDITH

I came to borrow a bicycle wrench.

ALICE

Listen to me a moment, will you?

JUDITH

Of course I will! [ALICE *sits on sofa.* JUDITH *remains standing.*] But don't beat about the bush. I don't like long homilies.

ALICE

Homilies? . . . Well, put your hair up and get into a long dress.

JUDITH

Why?

ALICE

Because you're not a child any longer! And you're too young to try and make yourself look younger still!

JUDITH

What does that mean?

ALICE

That you're old enough to get married! And the way you dress is making people talk!

JUDITH

Very well, I'll do it!

ALICE

You've understood, have you?

JUDITH

Yes.

ALICE

And we agree?

JUDITH

Completely!

ALICE

On all points?

JUDITH

Even the most sensitive!

ALICE

At the same time, will you stop playing fast and loose—with Allan?

JUDITH

This is really in earnest then?

ALICE

Yes!

JUDITH

Then we may as well start now.

> [*She has put down the handle-bars of the bicycle; now she lets down her cycling skirt, twists her plait into a knot, takes a hairpin from her mother's hair and fastens her knot.*]

ALICE

It's hardly the thing to do one's toilet in someone else's parlour!

JUDITH

Is this all right? . . . Then I'm ready! Come now who dares!

ALICE

At least you look respectable now! But leave Allan alone!

JUDITH

I don't understand what you mean by that.

ALICE

Can't you see how he's suffering? . . .

JUDITH

Yes, I think I have noticed it, but I don't know why. I'm not suffering.

ALICE

That's your strength! But wait . . . one day . . . oh yes, you'll know what it *is* to suffer! . . . Go home now and don't forget—you're wearing a long skirt.

JUDITH

Are you supposed to walk differently, then?

ALICE

Try!

JUDITH

[*trying to walk like a lady*] Oh! I've got a brake on my heels, I'm caught, I can't run any more!

ALICE

Yes, my child, the walk is beginning, the uphill road towards the unknown, which you know about already but have to pretend not to know! Shorter steps and slower, much slower! Children's shoes are finished for you, Judith. It's boots from now on. You don't remember when you stopped wearing baby socks and took to shoes, but *I* remember.

JUDITH

I'll never get used to this!

ALICE

But you must! You must!

> [JUDITH *goes up to her mother, gives her a quick kiss and goes out, very ladylike, completely forgetting the bicycle handle-bars.*]

JUDITH

Goodbye, Mother!

> [KURT *enters, left.*]

KURT

You're here already?

ALICE

Yes!

KURT

Has *he* come back?

ALICE

Yes! In dress uniform. So he must have called on the Colonel. Two decorations on his breast!

KURT

Two?—I knew he was due for the Order of the Sword when he retired. What can the other one be?

ALICE

I don't know. There was a white cross inside a red one.

KURT

That's Portuguese! . . . Let me think! . . . Look—didn't his articles
in the paper deal with Quarantine Stations in Portuguese harbours?

ALICE

Yes, as far as I can remember.

KURT

He's never been to Portugal, has he?

ALICE

Never!

KURT

But I have!

ALICE

Why do you talk so much when he's about? He's got sharp ears and
a very good memory.

KURT

Do you think Judith might have got him that decoration?

ALICE

Well, really—that's too much . . . [*getting up*] . . . you've gone too far
this time.

KURT

We're not going to squabble now, are we?

ALICE

That depends on you! Don't meddle with my affairs!

KURT

When they cut across mine I have to meddle with them, however
carefully I go about it. . . . Here *he* is!

ALICE

It's now that it's going to happen!

KURT

What is going to happen?

ALICE

You'll see!

KURT

I wish the attack would come because this state of siege has been getting on my nerves! I haven't a friend left on the whole island!

ALICE

Wait now! . . . Sit down here on this side . . . he'll be in the easy chair, then I can prompt you!

[THE CAPTAIN *enters, back, in full dress uniform, wearing the Order of the Sword and the Portuguese Order of Christ.*]

CAPTAIN

Good morning to you! So this is the trysting place!

ALICE

You're tired! Sit down! [THE CAPTAIN *sits down, contrary to expectation, on the sofa, left.*] Make yourself comfortable!

CAPTAIN

It's *very* comfortable here! You're too kind!

ALICE

[*to* KURT] Be careful, he's suspicious!

CAPTAIN

[*crossly*] What was that you said?

ALICE

[*to* KURT] He's been drinking.

CAPTAIN

[*roughly*] No, he hasn't! [*Silence.*] Well . . . how have you been amusing yourselves?

ALICE

And you?

CAPTAIN

Have you noticed my Orders?

ALICE

No!

CAPTAIN

I might have guessed. You're jealous. It's usual to congratulate people who have just been decorated.

ALICE

Oh, congratulations!

CAPTAIN

We're given this sort of thing instead of the laurel wreaths they heap on actresses!

ALICE

That's a dig at the wreaths on the walls of the tower at home. . . .

CAPTAIN

Which you got from your brother. . . .

ALICE
> Oh, shut up!

CAPTAIN
> And which I've had to bow and scrape to for twenty-five years . . .
> and which it has taken me twenty-five years to expose!

ALICE
> You've seen my brother?

CAPTAIN
> Frequently! [ALICE *is nonplussed.*] Well, Kurt! You're not very talka-
> tive, are you?

KURT
> I'm waiting!

CAPTAIN
> Listen! You've heard the big news, haven't you?

KURT
> No!

CAPTAIN
> Well, it's no pleasure for me to be the one who has to . . .

KURT
> Out with it, man!

CAPTAIN
> The soda factory has gone fut!

KURT
> That's terrible news!—How will it affect you?

CAPTAIN
> It won't! I sold out in time.

KURT
> That was clever of you.

CAPTAIN
> But how will it affect you?

KURT
> I'll be in a bad way.

CAPTAIN
> You've brought it all on yourself! You should have sold out in time, or
> bought the new shares.

KURT
> Then I'd have lost that money, too.

CAPTAIN
> No, you wouldn't! The company would have managed to stay afloat.

KURT
> You don't mean the company, you mean the Board. As far as I could

see, the new shares were a collection for the Board.

CAPTAIN

What you thought you saw won't save you from the wreck, will it?

KURT

No, I'll have to sell up everything I've got!

CAPTAIN

Everything?

KURT

Even the house and furniture!

CAPTAIN

That's terrible!

KURT

Worse things than that have happened to me!
[*Silence.*]

CAPTAIN

That's what happens when amateurs start gambling on the stock exchange.

KURT

Really! You know that if I hadn't subscribed I'd have been ostracized.
. . . "An additional source of income for the coastal population, for those whose livelihood depends on the sea, unlimited capital, unlimited as the sea itself . . . philanthropy and national prosperity. . . ." That's what you wrote and had printed! . . . And now you call it gambling!

CAPTAIN

[*unmoved*] What are you going to do now?

KURT

Have an auction, I suppose.

CAPTAIN

That would be the best thing.

KURT

What do you mean?

CAPTAIN

What I said! . . . [*Deliberately.*] Certain changes are going to be made here.

KURT

On the island?

CAPTAIN

Yes! . . . For instance . . . your official quarters are going to be exchanged for something more modest.

KURT

I see!

CAPTAIN

Well, the idea is to place the Quarantine Station on the periphery of the island, by the seashore.

KURT

My original idea!

CAPTAIN

[*dryly*] I know nothing about that. . . . I don't know your ideas on the subject. . . . However—it'll give you a good chance to get rid of your furniture now without attracting too much attention—the scandal, I mean!

KURT

What?

CAPTAIN

The scandal! [*Working himself up into a passion.*] Because it *is* a scandal to arrive at a new place and go bankrupt not long after you get there. It's not nice for the relatives . . . the relatives more than anyone!

KURT

It's worse still for me, isn't it?

CAPTAIN

I'll tell you one thing, my dear Kurt: if you hadn't had me on your side in this matter, you'd have been sent packing already.

KURT

That, too?

CAPTAIN

Yes. You're not as reliable as you ought to be! There have been complaints about your methods.

KURT

Justifiable ones?

CAPTAIN

I think so, because although you have some fine qualities, you're a bit slapdash—don't interrupt me—you're slapdash!

KURT

That's great!

CAPTAIN

However, the change I've told you about is going to take place quite soon. So I'd advise you to get the auction over at once or try to sell privately.

KURT

Privately? Where would I find a buyer here?

CAPTAIN

You're not suggesting that *I* should settle down in the middle of your furniture, are you? That *would* be nice! [*He shudders.*] Especially if you . . . think of what happened. . . .

KURT

And what was that? You mean what didn't happen, don't you?

CAPTAIN

[*turning*] Alice is so quiet. What's the matter with you, old girl? Out-of-sorts?

ALICE

I'm thinking. . . .

CAPTAIN

Fancy that! You're thinking? But you have to think quickly, correctly and clearly if it's to get you anywhere. So, think now! One, two, three! —Ha ha! You can't do it? . . . Well, then I will! . . . Where's Judith?

ALICE

Somewhere about!

CAPTAIN

Where's Allan? [ALICE *doesn't answer.*] Where's the Lieutenant? [ALICE *doesn't answer.*] Well, Kurt! What are you going to do with Allan now?

KURT

Do with him?

CAPTAIN

Yes, you can't afford to keep him in the Artillery, can you?

KURT

Probably not!

CAPTAIN

You'll have to try and get him into some cheap Infantry regiment up in Norrland or somewhere.

KURT

In Norrland?

CAPTAIN

Yes! Or let him get an office job. That's what I'd do if I were in your place . . . why not? [KURT *doesn't reply.*]
In these enlightened days! Well! . . . Alice is so exceptionally quiet! . . . Yes, my children, that is life's seesaw. One day you're on top looking arrogantly around, then you're as low as you can go, then up you go again! And so on! And that's the way it is! Yes! [*To* ALICE.] Did you say something? [ALICE *shakes her head.*]

CAPTAIN

We may expect guests here in a few days.

ALICE

Were you talking to *me?*

CAPTAIN

We may expect guests here in a few days! Distinguished guests!

ALICE

Who?

CAPTAIN

Oho! So you're interested! . . . You sit where you are and guess who's coming, and in between your guesses you can read this letter again. [*He hands her an open letter.*]

ALICE

My letter? Opened? Back from the post?

CAPTAIN

[*getting up*] Yes, as head of the family and your guardian, I must protect our sacred interests. I shall destroy, with an iron hand, any attempts to break the family ties through a criminal correspondence. Well? [ALICE *is cowed.*] I'm not dead, Alice, but don't get angry now, just when I'm going to raise us all out of this undeserved degradation, undeserved by me, at least!

ALICE

Judith! Judith!

CAPTAIN

And Holofernes? Is that me? Pooh! [*He goes out, back.*]

KURT

Who *is* this man?

ALICE

I don't know!

KURT

We're beaten!

ALICE

No doubt about that!

KURT

He's stripped me bare, but he's done it so cleverly that I can't accuse him of anything.

ALICE

Oh, no! He's made it look as though you owe him a great debt of gratitude.

KURT

Does he know what he's doing?

ALICE

No, I don't think he does. He follows his nature and his instincts and just now it seems as though he's on the right side when good luck and bad luck are being parceled out.

KURT

I suppose it's the Colonel who's coming.

ALICE

Probably! That's why Allan has to go!

KURT

You agree with that?

ALICE

Yes, I do!

KURT

Then our ways must part!

ALICE

[*getting ready to go*] For a time. But we'll meet again!

KURT

I imagine so.

ALICE

Do you know where?

KURT

Here!

ALICE

You've guessed then?

KURT

It's easy! He's going to get the house and buy the furniture with it!

ALICE

That's what I think! But don't desert me!

KURT

Not for a trifle like that!

ALICE

Goodbye! [*She goes out.*]

KURT

Goodbye!

Scene Three

The same. Outside it is cloudy and raining. ALICE *and* KURT *enter, back, wearing raincoats and carrying umbrellas.*

ALICE

So I've managed to get you here. . . . Kurt, I can't be so cruel as to say welcome to you in your own home. . . .

KURT

Why not? I've had three lots of bailiffs to deal with—and worse. This leaves me quite unmoved!

ALICE

Did *he* ask you to come here?

KURT

It was a formal summons, but on what grounds I don't know.

ALICE

He's not your chief, is he?

KURT

No, but he's set himself up as king of the island. If anyone stands up to him, he only has to mention the Colonel, and they all fall prostrate. Tell me, is it today the Colonel's coming?

ALICE

He's expected—but I don't know anything for certain—please sit down, won't you?

KURT

[*sitting down*] It looks just the same as it used to here.

ALICE

Don't think about it! Don't start the wound bleeding again.

KURT

The wound? I find it a bit strange, that's all! Strange—like the man himself! You know, when I first got to know him as a boy, I used to avoid him. . . . But he wouldn't leave me alone; used to flatter me, offered to help me, tried to get me in his debt. I still tried to avoid him but it was no good. . . . Now I'm his slave!

ALICE

Yes, but why? He should be in your debt, not you in his.

KURT

Since the bankruptcy, he's offered to help Allan get through his exam. . . .

ALICE

You'll pay dearly for it! . . . Do you still intend to stand for Parliament?

KURT

Yes. As far as I know, there's nothing against it.
          [*Silence.*]

ALICE

Is Allan really leaving today?

KURT

Yes, unless I can stop it!

ALICE

Well, it was nice while it lasted.

KURT

But it didn't last long—like everything else, except life . . . which lasts much too long.

ALICE

That's true! Won't you come in and wait in the drawing room? If they don't upset you, they upset me—these surroundings.

KURT

Just as you like!

ALICE

I feel ashamed. I feel so ashamed that I'd like to die, but I can't alter things.

KURT

Let's go then, shall we?

ALICE

Somebody's coming, anyway.
          [*They go out, left.* THE CAPTAIN *and* ALLAN *enter, back, both wearing uniforms and capes.*]

CAPTAIN

Sit down here, my boy, I want to talk to you. [ALLAN *sits down in the chair, left.*] It's raining today, otherwise I'd get a good view of the sea from here. [*Silence.*] Well? You don't want to leave, do you?

ALLAN

I'm sorry to leave my father!

CAPTAIN

Yes, your father! He's rather an unhappy man. [*Silence.*] Parents hardly ever know what's best for their children. There are exceptions, naturally. Hm! Listen, Allan! Do you hear from your mother?

ALLAN

Yes, she writes now and then.

CAPTAIN

You know she's your guardian?

ALLAN

Yes!

CAPTAIN

Now listen, Allan. Did you know that your mother had given me legal authority to act for her?

ALLAN

I didn't know that.

CAPTAIN

Well, you know it now! There can be no more discussion about your career. You're going to Norrland.

ALLAN

But I haven't the money. . . .

CAPTAIN

I've provided it.

ALLAN

In that case, I can only thank you, Uncle!

CAPTAIN

You're grateful, anyway. I can't say the same for others. Hm! [*Raising his voice.*] The Colonel . . . do you know the Colonel?

ALLAN

[*embarrassed*] No, I don't.

CAPTAIN

The Co-lo-nel [*stressing the word*] is my closest friend—[*hurries on*] as no doubt you know! Hm! The Colonel has interested himself in my family, including my wife's relatives. Through his good offices, the Colonel has managed to raise what funds are required for the completion of your course.—Now you know your obligations—and your father's—to the Colonel. . . . Have I made myself clear enough? [ALLAN *bows.*] Now go and do your packing. The money will be handed to

you at the gangway. Goodbye, my boy! [*Holds out a finger.*] Goodbye!
[*Gets up and goes out, right.*]

> [ALLAN, *left alone, looks round the room, very unhappy.*
> JUDITH *enters back. Her hair is up and she is beautifully
> dressed. She wears a long skirt and a hooded coat and carries
> an umbrella.*]

JUDITH

Allan?

ALLAN

[*turning round and gaping at* JUDITH] Is *that* Judith?

JUDITH

You don't recognize me? Where have you been all this time? . . .
What are you looking at? My long dress . . . and my hair. . . . You've
never seen it before! . . .

ALLAN

No!

JUDITH

I look like a woman now, don't I?
> [ALLAN *turns away from her.*]

JUDITH

[*seriously*] What are you doing here?

ALLAN

I've been saying goodbye!

JUDITH

What! Are you—leaving here?

ALLAN

I'm being posted to Norrland.

JUDITH

[*flabbergasted*] To Norrland?—When are you leaving?

ALLAN

Today!

JUDITH

Whose idea is this?

ALLAN

Your father's!

JUDITH

I thought so! [*She paces the room, stamping her feet.*] I wanted you to
stay here for today.

ALLAN

To meet the Colonel.

JUDITH

What do you know about the Colonel? . . . Is it quite definite that you're going?

ALLAN

I've no choice. And now I *want* to go.
                    [*Silence.*]

JUDITH

Why do you want to go now?

ALLAN

I want to get away from here. Out into the world!

JUDITH

It's too hemmed in here! Yes, Allan, I understand. It's unbearable here!—They speculate in soda and human beings!
[*Silence. With genuine emotion.*] Allan, you know I'm one of those lucky people who seem incapable of feeling suffering—but now I'm beginning to!

ALLAN

You?

JUDITH

Yes!—I'm beginning to now! [*She presses both her hands against her breast.*] Oh, how I'm suffering now! Oh! . . .

ALLAN

What's the matter?

JUDITH

I don't know—I'm stifling! I think I'm dying!

ALLAN

Judith?

JUDITH

[*crying*] Oh! . . . is *this* how it feels? Is this . . . poor boys!

ALLAN

I'd be laughing now if I were as cruel as you.

JUDITH

I'm not cruel; I didn't understand. . . . You mustn't go!

ALLAN

I must.

JUDITH

Go then! . . . But give me something to remember you by.

ALLAN

What have *I* to give you?

JUDITH

[*with deep feeling*] You! No, I'll never get over this! [*Crying and clasping her breast.*] I'm suffering now, I'm suffering. . . . What have you done to me? . . . I don't want to live any more!—Allan, don't go, not alone. We'll go together; we'll take the little boat, the little white one—and we'll sail off, with the sheet made fast—there's a good wind . . . and we'll go on and on till we founder—out there, right out there, where there's no seaweed to tangle us up and no jellyfish—Well? What do you say? But we should have washed the sails yesterday—they should be snow-white—at that moment, I only want to see pure white—and then you'll swim, with me in your arms till you're tired out—and we'll sink. . . . [*Turns.*] That would be magnificent! Much finer than going around here with tears in my eyes, trying to smuggle out letters that Father will open and laugh to scorn! Allan! [*She grabs his arms and shakes him.*] Are you listening?

ALLAN

[*who has been looking at her with shining eyes*] Judith! Judith! Why didn't you tell me this before?

JUDITH

I didn't know. How could I tell you what I didn't know?

ALLAN

And now I've got to leave you! . . . But I suppose it's the best thing, the only thing to do! . . . I can't compete with a man . . . like . . .

JUDITH

Don't mention the Colonel to me!

ALLAN

Isn't it true?

JUDITH

Well—yes and no!

ALLAN

Can't it be "No" and nothing else?

JUDITH

Yes, it can. In an hour, it will!

ALLAN

Will you keep your word? I can wait, I can wait till . . . I can work! . . . Judith!

JUDITH

Don't go yet!—How long must I wait?

ALLAN

A year.

JUDITH

[*shouting for joy*] A year? I'll wait a thousand years, and if you're not back by then, I'll turn the heavens inside out so that the sun will rise

in the west. . . . Ssh! Somebody's coming!—Allan, we must part. . . .
Quiet!—Take me in your arms. [*They embrace.*] But you mustn't
kiss me. [*Turns her head away.*] Go now, will you—go!

> [ALLAN *goes to back and puts on his cape. Then they rush
> into each other's arms so that* JUDITH *disappears inside his
> cape. For a moment they kiss, then* ALLAN *runs out, back.*
> JUDITH *throws herself face down on the sofa, sobbing.* ALLAN
> *returns and kneels by her.*]

ALLAN

No, I can't go! I can't leave you now. Not now!

JUDITH

[*getting up*] If you only knew how beautiful you are now! If you could
only see yourself!

ALLAN

Be quiet! A man can't be beautiful! But you, Judith! You—that you—
I can see that when you are kind, there's another Judith . . . and she's
mine! . . . But if you throw me over, I'll die!

JUDITH

I think I'm dying, anyway! I want to die, now, this very moment, when
I'm so happy. . . .

ALLAN

Somebody's coming!

JUDITH

Let them come! I'm not afraid of anything in the whole world now!
But I wish you'd take me with you under your cape. [*She tries hiding
herself under the cape.*] I'll fly with you to Norrland. What shall we
do in Norrland? Join the Rifle Brigade . . . the one with feathers in
their hats. . . . It's very stylish and it'll suit you so well.

[*She plays with his hair.* ALLAN *kisses her fingers, one after the other,
then he kisses one of her boots.*] What are you doing, you madman?
You'll make your mouth all black! [*Gets up hurriedly.*] And then I
won't be able to kiss you, when you go! Come on, I'm going with you!

ALLAN

No, I'll be arrested.

JUDITH

Then I'll join you in the guardroom!

ALLAN

They wouldn't allow it. We must part now.

JUDITH

I'll swim after the steamer . . . and you'll dive in and save me, and it'll
get in the papers, and we'll get engaged! Shall we do that?

ALLAN

You can still joke then?

JUDITH

There's always time to cry. . . . Say goodbye now. . . .

> [*They are in each other's arms, then* ALLAN *goes out through the open French windows at back. They embrace outside in the rain.*]

ALLAN

You're getting wet. Judith!

JUDITH

What do I care!

> [*They tear themselves away.* ALLAN *goes,* JUDITH *stays there in the wind and rain which make sport of her hair and her clothes, while she waves her handkerchief. Then she rushes in and throws herself on the sofa, her face hidden in her hands.* ALICE *enters and goes up to her.*]

ALICE

What's the matter? . . . Are you ill?—Get up and let me see.

> [JUDITH *sits up.*]

ALICE

[*looking at her intently*] You're not ill! And you'll get no sympathy from me! [*Goes out, right.*]

> [THE LIEUTENANT *enters, back.* JUDITH *stands up and puts on her hooded coat.*]

JUDITH

Would you come to the telegraph office with me, Lieutenant?

LIEUTENANT

If I can be of any service to you . . . but I don't think it's quite the thing. . . .

JUDITH

All the better! It's what I want . . . you to compromise me . . . but don't get any wrong ideas. Lead the way!

> [*They go out, back.* THE CAPTAIN *and* ALICE *enter, right.* THE CAPTAIN *is in undress uniform. He sits on the easy chair.*]

CAPTAIN

Tell him he may come in.

> [ALICE *goes left, and opens the door, then she sits down on the sofa.* KURT *enters, left.*]

KURT

You sent for me?

CAPTAIN

[*friendly but a little condescending*] Yes, I've several important things to tell you! Sit down!

[KURT *sits down on the chair, left.*]

KURT

I'm all ears!

CAPTAIN

Well, to start with. . . . [*Arrogantly.*] You know that the quarantine system here has been going from bad to worse for the last hundred years or so . . .

ALICE

[*to* KURT] It's the candidate for Parliament who's speaking now.

CAPTAIN

. . . but—thanks to the spectacular development recently in . . .

ALICE

[*to* KURT] Communications, of course!

CAPTAIN

. . . so many directions, the Government is planning to widen its scope. With that in mind, the Ministry of Health has appointed inspectors—and . . .

ALICE

[*to* KURT] He's practicing dictation. . . .

CAPTAIN

You'll hear about it anyway, so it's as well now as later. *I* have been appointed Quarantine Inspector!

[*Silence.*]

KURT

My congratulations! And while I'm about it, my homage, too!

CAPTAIN

In view of our family ties, our personal relationship will not be affected. However—there's something else to talk about. At my request, your son Allan has been transferred to an Infantry regiment in Norrland.

KURT

But I don't want him to go to Norrland.

CAPTAIN

What you want in this matter must be subordinated to what his mother wants . . . and, as his mother has authorized me to decide for her . . . I have decided.

KURT

I admire you.

CAPTAIN

Is that your only feeling at the very moment you're going to part from your son? Haven't you any real human feelings?

KURT

You mean—I should be suffering?

CAPTAIN

Yes.

KURT

You'd like to see me suffering. . . . You want me to *show how* I'm suffering?

CAPTAIN

You *can't* suffer, can you? . . . I remember once when I was taken ill, and you were in the room. Your expression showed how pleased you were. You couldn't hide it.

ALICE

That's not true! Kurt sat by your bed the whole night and calmed you down when your pangs of conscience were too much for you—but the moment you got better, you stopped being grateful. . . .

CAPTAIN

[*pretending not to hear* ALICE] So Allan will be leaving us.

KURT

Who's paying for all this?

CAPTAIN

I've arranged it already . . . that is to say, we, a syndicate, who have taken an interest in the young man's future.

KURT

Syndicate?

CAPTAIN

Yes! And if you want to satisfy yourself that it's all above board, you can scan the subscription lists here. [*Hands him some sheets of paper.*]

KURT

Lists? [*Reads the sheets of paper.*] Are these begging letters?

CAPTAIN

You could call them that!

KURT

Have you been begging on my son's behalf?

CAPTAIN

There you are! Ingratitude again! An ungrateful man is the heaviest burden the earth can carry.

KURT

That's the end of me socially! And of my hopes for Parliament!

CAPTAIN

Hopes for what?

KURT

For Parliament!

CAPTAIN

You haven't been aspiring to that, have you? Especially as it must have dawned on you that I might stand myself. I *am* senior to you. You seem to have underestimated me.

KURT

So it's goodbye to that, too!

CAPTAIN

You don't seem worried unduly.

KURT

You've taken everything from me now. Is there anything else you want?

CAPTAIN

What else have you got? Is there anything you can reproach me for? Think carefully! Is there anything you can reproach me for?
[*Silence.*]

KURT

Strictly speaking, nothing. You've kept inside the law. Everything has been done correctly as between honest citizens in their daily life. . . .

CAPTAIN

You said that with a sort of resignation I can only call cynical. But your whole nature has a tendency to cynicism, my dear Kurt, and there are times when I am tempted to share Alice's opinion of you— that you are a hypocrite, a first-rate hypocrite!

KURT

[*calmly*] Is that Alice's opinion?

ALICE

[*to* KURT] It was once. But not any more. To go through what you have gone through needs real courage or—something else.

CAPTAIN

I think the discussion may now be regarded as closed. You'd better go and say goodbye to Allan. He's leaving by the next steamer.

KURT

[*getting up*] So soon? . . . Well! I've been through worse!

CAPTAIN

You say that so often that I've begun to wonder what you *did* go through in America.

KURT

Go through? One misfortune after another. But to suffer misfortunes is the undisputed right of the whole human race.

CAPTAIN

[*sharply*] Some people bring misfortunes on themselves. Were yours that sort?

KURT

Isn't that a rather delicate question, a question of conscience?

CAPTAIN

[*shortly*] Have *you* got a conscience?

KURT

There are wolves and there are sheep; no one need be proud of being a sheep. But I'd rather be that than a wolf!

CAPTAIN

Don't you know the old truth that a man's fate is in his own hands?

KURT

Is *that* a truth?

CAPTAIN

And don't you know that a man's own strength . . .

KURT

Yes, I learned *that* the night your own strength failed you and you were flat out on the floor!

CAPTAIN

[*raising his voice*] A man of merit like me, me here—yes, look at me —for fifty years I struggled against a whole world but at last I've won through because of perseverance, duty, energy and—integrity!

ALICE

You should leave that for others to say!

CAPTAIN

Others won't because others are jealous! However!—We're expecting guests. My daughter, Judith is going to meet her future husband. . . . Where *is* Judith?

ALICE

Out!

CAPTAIN

In the rain? . . . Send for her!

KURT

May I go now?

CAPTAIN

No, stay where you are! . . . Is Judith dressed? Decently?

ALICE

Good enough. . . . Is it absolutely certain that the Colonel's coming?

CAPTAIN

[*getting up*] It's absolutely certain that he's going to take us by surprise. . . . I'm expecting his telegram—any minute now! [*Goes in, right.*] Back in a minute!

ALICE

There he is—the whole man! Is he human?

KURT

When you asked me that before, I said no. Now I believe he's typical of so many who possess the earth. . . . Perhaps we're a little bit like that, too? Using people for our own ends and never missing an opportunity of doing it!

ALICE

He's eaten you and yours alive . . . and you defend him?

KURT

I tell you I've been through worse. . . . But this man-eater has left my soul alone. He could never feed on that.

ALICE

What "worse" have you been through?

KURT

You are asking me?

ALICE

Are you trying to be offensive?

KURT

I'm trying *not* to be . . . so don't ask me again.
[THE CAPTAIN *enters, right.*]

CAPTAIN

The telegram was here already. Read it please, will you, Alice—my sight's not so good. [*Sits down, very important, in the easy chair.*] Read it! Don't go, Kurt!
[ALICE *scans it quickly and looks dumbfounded.*]

CAPTAIN

Well? Aren't you pleased about it?
[ALICE *remains silent, just staring at* THE CAPTAIN.]

CAPTAIN

[*ironically*] Well, who's it from?

ALICE

It's from the Colonel.

CAPTAIN

[*pleased*] There you are! And what does the Colonel say?

ALICE

He says "Because of Miss Judith's impudent telephone message, I consider our relationship ended—for ever." [*Stares hard at* THE CAPTAIN.]

CAPTAIN

Read it again—will you?

ALICE

[*reading quickly*] "Because of Miss Judith's impudent telephone message, I regard our relationship ended—for ever."

CAPTAIN

[*turning pale*] She *is* Judith!

ALICE

And you are Holofernes!

CAPTAIN

Who are you then?

ALICE

You'll soon see!

CAPTAIN

This is your doing!

ALICE

No!

CAPTAIN

[*livid*] This is your doing!

ALICE

No!

> [THE CAPTAIN *tries to get up and draw his sword, but falls back, helpless.*]

ALICE

Now you've got your deserts!

CAPTAIN

[*moaning, his voice senile*] Don't be angry with me! I'm a sick man!

ALICE

Are you? I'm glad to hear it!

KURT

Let's get him to bed.

ALICE

No, I won't touch him! [*Rings bell.*]

CAPTAIN

[*as before*] You mustn't be angry with me. [*To* KURT.] Take care of my children.

KURT

This is sublime! *I* am to take care of his children, and *he* has stolen mine!

ALICE

This aberration of his!

CAPTAIN

Take care of my children. [*He goes on mumbling incoherently.*]

ALICE

At last that tongue is stopped!—It can't brag any more, nor lie any
more, nor wound any more. You, Kurt, you believe in God! Thank
Him for me! Thank Him for freeing me from the tower, from the
wolf, from the vampire!

CAPTAIN

Alice, please. . . .

ALICE

[*close to* THE CAPTAIN's *face*] Where's your strength now? Where is
it? And your energy? [THE CAPTAIN, *speechless, spits in her face.*] You
can still spit venom, you viper! Then I'll have to tear your tongue out!
[*She slaps his face.*] The head is cut off, but it can still blush! . . . Oh,
Judith, my glorious girl, I bore you under my heart like an Angel of
Vengeance and you've set us free, all of us!—Have you any more
heads, you Hydra? Then we'll take them, too! [*Pulling his beard.*]
Now I know there *is* justice on earth! Sometimes, I've dreamt about it,
but I've never believed it. Kurt, will you ask God to forgive me for
misjudging Him. Yes, justice exists! I'll become one of His sheep now!
Tell Him that, Kurt! A bit of good fortune makes us better beings; it's
constant misfortune that turns us into wolves!

[THE LIEUTENANT *enters, back.*]

ALICE

The Captain has had a stroke; will you help us get the chair out,
please?

LIEUTENANT

Madam . . .

ALICE

What's the matter?

LIEUTENANT

Well, Miss Judith . . .

ALICE

Help us here, first! You can tell us about Miss Judith later! [THE
LIEUTENANT *wheels the chair out, right.*] Out with the carcass! Out
with it and open all the doors wide! It's fresh air we need in here!
[*Opens the French windows. It has cleared up outside.*] Aaah!

KURT

Are you going to abandon him?

ALICE

Everyone abandons a sinking ship. The crew save themselves! I don't have to lay out a putrifying brute! Let the pathologist have him or the mortuary! A garden plot would be too good for that barrow-load of filth! . . . Now I'm going to have a bath to get rid of all this dirt,—if I can ever be clean again!

[JUDITH *is seen outside by the balustrade, bareheaded, waving her handkerchief towards the sea.*]

KURT

[*going out, back*] Who's there? Judith! [*Shouts.*] Judith!

JUDITH

[*entering, in tears*] He's gone!

KURT

Who?

JUDITH

Allan's gone!

KURT

Without saying goodbye?

JUDITH

We said goodbye and he sent you his love, Uncle!

ALICE

Oh, was that it?

JUDITH

[*throwing herself into* KURT's *arms*] He's gone!

KURT

He'll be back, my child!

ALICE

Or we'll go after him!

KURT

[*with a gesture towards the door, right*] And leave him? . . . What would people . . . ?

ALICE

People! Bah! . . . Judith, come and kiss me! [JUDITH *goes to* ALICE, *who kisses her forehead.*] Do you want to go after him?

JUDITH

How can you ask?

ALICE

But your father's ill!

JUDITH

I don't care!

ALICE

That's my Judith! Oh, I love you, Judith!

JUDITH

Besides, Papa isn't mean . . . and he doesn't like being pampered! Papa has something grand about him!

ALICE

Yes, I suppose he has.

JUDITH

And I don't think he'll want to see me after that telephone message. . . . Why did he try to foist that old man on me? No, Allan, Allan! [*Throws herself into* KURT's *arms.*] I want to go to Allan! [*Tears herself away again and runs out to wave.* KURT *follows her and waves, too.*]

ALICE

To think that flowers can grow out of dirt! [LIEUTENANT *enters, right.*] Well?

LIEUTENANT

Well, Miss Judith . . .

ALICE

Is her name so sweet on your lips that you forget there's a man dying?

LIEUTENANT

Yes, but she said . . .

ALICE

She? Say Judith if you prefer it. . . . But first, how is he—in there?

LIEUTENANT

Oh, in there? . . . It's all over!

ALICE

Over?—Oh God, for myself and all mankind, I thank Thee for delivering us from this evil! . . . Give me your arm! I want to go out and breathe—breathe! [THE LIEUTENANT *gives her his arm.* ALICE *stops.*] Did he say anything before he died?

LIEUTENANT

Yes, Miss Judith's father did say a few words.

ALICE

What were they?

LIEUTENANT

He said "Forgive them, for they know not what they do."

ALICE

Unbelievable!

LIEUTENANT

Miss Judith's father was a good man, a noble man.

ALICE

Kurt! [KURT *enters.*] It's all over!

KURT

Oh! . . .

ALICE

Do you know what his last words were? No, you don't. "Forgive them, for they know not what they do."

KURT

Can you decipher that one?

ALICE

I suppose he meant that *he* had always done the right thing and that he died wronged by life.

KURT

They'll give him a wonderful funeral oration!

ALICE

And lots of wreaths! From the N.C.O.'s. . . .

KURT

Oh, yes!

ALICE

A year ago he said something about life being a huge joke.

KURT

You mean he was poking fun at us right till the end?

ALICE

No! . . . But now, when he's dead, I feel a strange urge to speak well of him!

KURT

Well then, let's do it!

LIEUTENANT

Miss Judith's father was a good man, a noble man!

ALICE

[*to* KURT] There you are!

KURT

"They know not what they do." How many times did I ask you if he knew what he was doing? And you thought he didn't know! So, forgive him!

ALICE

Riddles! . . . Riddles! . . . But there's peace in the house now! The wonderful peace of death! Wonderful as the solemn awe we feel when a child is coming into the world! I can hear the silence . . . and on the floor I can see the lines of the easy chair that took him away. And I feel now that my own life is over and that I'm on the way to the grave.

Do you know, it's strange, but those simple words of the Lieutenant— and he is a simple man—I can still hear them—and they've become real now. My husband, the loved one of my youth—yes, laugh if you like—he *was* a good man, a noble man—despite everything!

KURT

Despite everything. He was a brave man—the way he fought for himself and his family!

ALICE

The frustrations! The humiliations! And he wiped the slate clean— so that he could pass on.

KURT

He was one who was *passed by*! And that says everything! Alice, go in to him!

ALICE

No, I can't. While we've been talking here, the image of him as he was in his youth has come back to me. I saw him, I can see him now, as he was when he was twenty years old! . . . I must have loved that man!

KURT

And hated!

ALICE

And hated! . . . God rest his soul! [*Goes towards the door, right, and stays there, her hands clasped.*]

A NOTE ON THE TRANSLATOR

Norman Ginsbury is both a successful playwright and an accomplished translator. Born in 1902 in London, and an Honours graduate of London University, Mr. Ginsbury has become well-known to theatregoers. Among his plays are *The First Gentleman,* which ran for nearly 700 performances in London, *Viceroy Sarah,* which was directed by Tyrone Guthrie, *Walk in the Sun, The Gambler,* which he is now turning into a musical, *My Dear Isabella, The School for Rivals* (for the Bath Festival), *Take Back Your Freedom, The Happy Man, The First Comers* (for the Festival of Britain), and many more.

In addition to his new translation of Strindberg's *Dance of Death,* Mr. Ginsbury's translations of a number of Henrik Ibsen's plays have been produced including *Ghosts, A Doll's House, An Enemy of the People, Rosmersholm, Pillars of Society,* and *Peer Gynt.* Tyrone Guthrie directed the Norman Ginsbury *Peer Gynt* at the Old Vic Theatre in London with a cast which included Ralph Richardson, Sybil Thorndike, Laurence Olivier, Margaret Leighton and Joyce Redman.

Norman Ginsbury lives with his wife Sarah in Eastbourne, Sussex, England.

A NOTE ON THE DESIGN

Tyrone Guthrie Theatre Editions have been designed for maximum legibility and convenience in reading.

The text of this book was set in Fairfield, a typeface designed by Rudolph Ruzicka and considered one of the finest ever cut for book work. Fairfield is not seen often because few books still are printed by letterpress on the soft papers for which this graceful type was intended.

Type composition of the books in this edition is by Dahl & Curry, Inc. of Minneapolis. The books were printed by Lund Press, Smyth sewn and bound by the A. J. Dahl Company, both of Minneapolis. Paper manufactured by West Virginia Pulp & Paper Company.